THE WALL
IN MY
BACKYARD

To Hunter-Bernards,
Thank you so much
for your friendship. All
the best, Dinah

The Wall in My Backyard

EAST GERMAN WOMEN IN TRANSITION

Edited by

Dinah Dodds

and

Pam Allen-Thompson

Interviews and Translation by Dinah Dodds

University of Massachusetts Press
Amherst

Copyright © 1994 by
The University of Massachusetts Press
All rights reserved
Printed in the United States of America
LC 94-18664
ISBN 0-87023-932-5 (cloth); 933-3 (pbk.)
Designed by Jack Harrison
Set in Adobe Minion by Keystone Typesetting, Inc.
Printed and bound by Thomson-Shore, Inc.

Library of Congress Cataloging-in-Publication Data
The wall in my backyard : East German women in transition / edited by
   Dinah Dodds and Pam Allen-Thompson ; interviews and translation by
   Dinah Dodds.
       p.   cm.
   Includes bibliographical references.
       ISBN 0–87023–932–5 (alk. paper). — ISBN 0–87023–933–3 (pbk. :
   alk. paper)
       1. Women—Germany (East)—Social conditions.
       2. Women—Germany (East)—Interviews.   3. Germany (East)—Social conditions.
   I. Dodds, Dinah Jane, 1943–   .   II. Allen-Thompson, Pam, 1954–
   HQ1630.5.W35   1994
   305.42′09431—dc20   94–18664
                          CIP

British Library Cataloguing in Publication data are available.

The interview with Helga Schütz appeared as "Die Mauer stand bei mir im Garten," in *Women in German Yearbook 7: Feminist Studies in German Literature and Culture*, ed. Jeanette Clausen and Sara Friedrichsmeyer. Copyright 1991 by the University of Nebraska Press. Used by permission of the publisher.

*"I lived for eighteen years with
the Wall in my backyard"*

—HELGA SCHÜTZ

CONTENTS

ACKNOWLEDGMENTS

Deepest gratitude goes to the twenty-six East Berlin women who were interviewed for this book, including the eight whose interviews could not be included here. They generously shared their time and their stories. This book was possible only because they had the courage to speak candidly about their personal lives.

A number of other people deserve special thanks for their contribution to this volume. Kathleen Bogan accompanied me to Berlin during the fall of 1990 on a Fulbright Faculty Research Grant. A gifted writer and editor, she spent many hours reading the manuscript and making suggestions about organization and clarity. I am grateful to Portland author Floyd Skloot for the initial encouragement to publish the interviews. My colleague Angela Jung, director of the Lewis and Clark College study-abroad program in Munich, provided the initial interview contacts. Ginga Eichler, who was employed at the Agency for Foreigners in the East Berlin *Magistrat,* introduced me to others while I worked from her East Berlin city-center apartment. Actress Vera Oelschlegel offered her home on Müggel Lake in East Berlin as a base for the final editing.

I am particularly grateful to Pam Allen-Thompson, German Studies scholar and Research Professor for Women's Studies at the University of Toledo, for giving this book the benefit of her skill as a writer and her expertise on the history and culture of the German Democratic Republic. Her knowledge provided valuable context for the introduction which she drafted, as well as for the bibliography which she prepared. In the countless hours of editing together, she and I discovered the satisfaction of collaborative work, talking through our differing opinions until we found agreement.

Financial support for this project came from Lewis and Clark College in Portland, Oregon, which granted me a sabbatical leave to Berlin during the fall and winter of 1990–1991 and a travel grant to return in the summer of 1992. Research grants were provided to Pam Allen-Thompson by the German Academic Exchange Service (DAAD), and by the Ohio State University Center for Women's Studies, which administered the Elizabeth Gee Grant for Research on Women.

DINAH DODDS

THE WALL
IN MY
BACKYARD

INTRODUCTION

Pam Allen-Thompson
and Dinah Dodds

I

The radical changes that occurred in the German Democratic Republic (GDR) with the opening of the Berlin Wall in November 1989 ushered in a period of chaotic transition for the East German people. The collapse of the forty-year-old government of the Socialist Unity Party (SED), the speedy economic and political unification with the Federal Republic of Germany (FRG), the abrupt switch from a centrally planned economy to a social market economy, and the complicated restructuring of all social and political institutions marked one of the most far-reaching turning points of modern European history. The enormous psychological adjustment accompanying each of these processes, including the overnight change of citizenship for sixteen million people, cannot be easily comprehended. Indeed, the more extensive the study of this transition—called in German the "*Wende*," or turn—the greater the sense of its complexity.

This book is a collection of interviews with eighteen women who experienced that automatic change of citizenship. In the interviews the women touch upon numerous aspects of life in the former GDR, the territory now referred to as the five new federal states. They depict the excitement and frustration of the rapid and radical changes that followed the lifting of travel restrictions and the opening of the Wall. They also tell how their lives were affected by the social and political changes of German unification.

The book's focus, however, is women's issues, as the interviewees discuss candidly and critically some of the problems they faced as women. Because the GDR proclaimed legal equality for women, the editors wanted to know whether these women perceived themselves as equal to men in their society. We were interested, too, in learning how the women evaluated the GDR's *Frauenpolitik,* or policies that applied specifically to women.

The backdrop against which the women told their stories was the turmoil of the *Wende,* a time period so chaotic that there is no full agreement on when the *Wende* actually began. The most commonly accepted date is November 9, 1989, when Günter Schabowski, Party Secretary for Information, unexpectedly announced on the evening news during the Tenth Plenum of the Central Committee that permission to cross the border would now be given on short notice, and that travel requests would be denied only in exceptional cases. A few hours later thousands had crossed the border from East Berlin into West Berlin. In the following weeks, millions traveled from the GDR into the West (*Chronik* 20).

For some East Germans, the *Wende* is marked by the demonstrations on the occasion of the fortieth anniversary of the GDR, October 7, 1989. These protests were inspired by the Monday night peace vigils that started in Leipzig in the early 1980s and grew to massive demonstrations for democratic reform during the fall of 1989. The October 7 protest demonstrations were organized in defiance of the staged annual parades that commemorated the GDR's anniversary and were met in major cities with police brutality and many arrests. In the minds of some, the widespread beatings signaled the end of the GDR as a reformable state and, as such, the real *Wende.*

Some East Germans prefer to mark the *Wende* earlier with the opening of the Hungarian border in May 1989, which initiated the exodus of one million East Germans before the Wall was opened. Others give credit for the *Wende* to Soviet leader Mikhail Gorbachev, reaching back to his accession to power in 1985 or to the (late) advent of *glasnost* in the GDR in 1988. Still others prefer not to use the term *Wende* at all, arguing that nothing really happened other than the exchange of one authoritarian government for another.

As the final chapter in the history of the GDR, the *Wende* provides an occasion for reflection and appraisal. Some GDR citizens have reacted to the turmoil of the *Wende* with critical introspection about their own responsibility in perpetuating the system; others have blamed outside forces for their suffering. This time of transition provides a unique opportunity for looking into the complexity of GDR society. As cultural theorists have pointed out, societal analysis can be most productive in times of upheaval when patterns are interrupted, expectations disappointed, and values challenged. The study of a society in flux can reveal more about the subtle characteristics of daily life than can a reading of a society fixed comfortably in its status quo.

The first set of interviews was conducted from two to five months after political unification on October 3, 1990. They document thoughts and experiences from the early phase of the transition period. Enough time had passed to give some indication of the changes brought by unification, and memories of the chaos following the opening of the borders were still fresh. Other significant moments in GDR history as well as experiences from the period immediately following World War II are also recalled. A second set of interviews was conducted in July 1992. Summaries of these follow-up conversations document some of the changes in these women's lives one and a half years later. Here the period reflected upon is the time after the milestone events of autumn 1989.

The voices heard here counter stale stereotypes and emerging myths, which—though they may contain some degree of truth—limit a full understanding of this culture. The stories these women tell call for a rethinking of previously held notions about what East German women really gained in the emancipation that was dictated to them, as well as what they lost in the unification that was forged for them. Although many viewed a vote for the conservative CDU coalition in the first all-German elections as a vote of support for unification, no vote on unification as such was ever held. By challenging the misconception that life in the GDR was monolithic, the book attempts to contribute to an understanding of the complexity of this transition.

II

The interview as source material has a long-standing tradition in numerous academic disciplines, particularly in the social sciences. In societies where the expression of opinion is restricted, however, interview data are not readily accessible. For that reason, empirical research based on interviews existed in the GDR only within the limitations of state control. It is ironic, then, that the interview genre played a significant albeit sporadic role in the literature of that country.

The contribution of GDR authors to the interview genre was examined by Germanist Albrecht Holschuh, who suggests that Sarah Kirsch broke new ground in 1972 with her book of taped narratives from five GDR women, *The Panther Woman*. Maxie Wander's *Good Morning, You Beauty*—a volume of interviews with East German women who spoke candidly about their lives in the GDR, including taboo subjects such as sexuality—followed five years later and, in spite of limited availability, was widely read in the GDR. This and subsequent interview publications served as a form of substitute journalism in the absence of a free press. Holschuh's analysis also speaks to the primary problem of interview projects, which is the tendency of the readership to accept published interviews as authentic, factual confessions and memoirs—much in the tradition of letters and diaries—without taking into account the role of the editor in shaping the information presented (267). This shaping takes place first through the editor's selection and formulation of questions, which determine to a great degree the topics discussed. Next, the editor establishes certain criteria for selecting the interviewees. In addition, the unseen hand of the editor cuts and pastes by including that part of the interview that she or he finds most interesting or most supportive of the editorial intent. Similarly, the editor might arrange the contents of the interview to make for smoother reading or to give ideological emphasis. In some cases, the editor might even add text in an attempt to better express an interviewee's intentions (Holschuh 278–79).

Accepting that an inherent authorial bias exists in documentary work of any kind, including interview projects, we acknowledge that our goal in compiling this collection of interviews was to suggest a more differentiated picture of women's experience in the GDR than what was widely available in either the East or the West. The official Party portrayal of women showed zealous mothers who mastered both work and family out of love for their socialist fatherland. The Western media depicted them as oppressed, downtrodden, locked-in people who were often reduced to "the spies" and "the spied-on," while leftist intellectuals maintained that East German women were generally more emancipated than their peers in the West. In choosing to let a small group of women speak for themselves, we ask readers to complete the project by formulating their own opinions about what life might have been like for these women.

The process of moving from the oral text to the printed page involved a number of steps. The first set of interviews was conducted, transcribed, and translated by Dinah Dodds. The follow-up interviews, also conducted by Dodds, were noted on paper rather than recorded on tape. The interview transcriptions were then edited by Dinah Dodds and Pam Allen-Thompson. As North Americans, we worked with the interview material from the position of outsiders. Even with professional training in GDR history and culture and extensive stays in the country both before and after the opening of the Wall, we acknowledge that an outsider cannot fully understand what life was like in the GDR. Nevertheless, we have drawn from our combined experience to facilitate for a generalist audience an understanding of this complex culture.

Following our own editing, the women interviewed were given the opportunity to revise the transcriptions of their conversations. Most speakers left the written text exactly as it stood, and some made minor additions for clarification. In one instance a page of text was deleted because the mother of one of the interviewees felt that the information might be incriminating to her. Four women asked that only the first name and last initial be used, while one woman asked for a pseudonym.

The interviewees were selected using a variety of methods: seeking out persons actively involved with women's issues, that is, those working in the newly formed women's organizations and in local, regional, and national politics; referrals to women in other occupations such as medicine, unskilled labor, self-employment, academia, and the arts; and chance encounters that occurred while Dodds was living in eastern Berlin between December 1990 and April 1991. Neither of the editors was personally acquainted with any of the women interviewed.

The group consisted of women with and without children, as well as women in a variety of partner arrangements, for example, un-partnered, with a same-sex partner, or with an opposite-sex partner. Some interviewees were still married to the original partner, while others had been divorced once or several times. Ages ranged from twenty to sixty-nine, but women in their forties and fifties predominated.

Of the original twenty-six interviews, we selected eighteen for the book, choosing those that expressed the widest variety of perspectives on women's issues. We also wanted to avoid overrepresentation of any one professional group. For example, of the interviews with two writers and two students, only one of each was chosen; of interviews with seven academics, two were included—a researcher at the Academy of Sciences and a retired professor who was active in women's issues.

The search for occupational distribution turned up members of various minority groups, including professing Christians, lesbians, and GDR citizens of other national origins. Still, not every minority faction could be represented, nor is any group represented in proportion to its demographic distribution within the population. Some groups are unfortunately not represented at all. Voices from small towns or rural areas, for example, are completely absent. Even though a number of the interviewees did not grow up in Berlin, all had been living there for some time. The inherent advantages of having resided in the capital city of the GDR—with all the supporting institutions that made this city the showcase of socialist Germany—provided these women with a different experience from those living in other cities or in the country. The urban flavor of this collection of interviews as well as the disproportionately high percentage of well-educated women means, too, that professionals are overrepresented, and that most of the group are relatively privileged.

The inclusion of a particular interview does not suggest that the interviewee is representative of any of the many "tags" she wears. That is to say, the filmmaker does not speak for all filmmakers, nor does the physical therapist speak for all physical therapists. Mothers do not speak for other mothers. However, many of the experiences and opinions related here are in some ways typical. This collection of interviews conveys something of the range and uniqueness of individual experience within the former GDR and, at the same time, gives a sense of the commonalities of the cultural environment.

The speakers vary in their degree of directness and openness, their level of emotional involvement, their ability to articulate their thoughts and feelings, and their familiarity with the *Frauenpolitik* in the GDR and the FRG. Inaccuracies in matters of GDR social policy were not edited from the interviews. Instead, we provide documented background on GDR laws and practices in section III of this introduction to aid interpretation of the interviews. Committed to allowing each of these women to speak for herself, we made no attempt to rectify the ambiguities and differences found in the texts. Contradictory viewpoints, such as the role Party membership played in securing privilege, are left intact.

As would be expected, this diverse group exhibits differing views on a variety of issues. For example, a physical therapist insisted that yoga was prohibited in the GDR, while another interviewee mentioned that she took part in an officially sanctioned yoga workshop at a GDR health spa. In another instance, one woman made an award-winning film that showed German and Soviet children learning each other's language by playing together, while another woman complained that in her apartment complex, the German children repeatedly refused to allow the Russian children to enter the playground. Diverging opinions surrounded the topic of the advantages and disadvantages of taking small babies to day care.

The interviewees also experienced the changes in their everyday lives in different ways. One lamented her full schedule since the *Wende,* which no longer allowed her to read books. Another was thrilled with the conveniences brought by the new system, happy that she could read books again for the first time since childhood. Referring to the social acceptance of children born outside of wedlock, a woman who was reared by an unmarried mother volunteered that she had suffered no discrimination because of it, but a mother who was herself unmarried insisted that many people had discriminated against her: after the birth of her child she was called a whore by her own family. This story is consistent with that of a young mother who said that, to avoid this discrimination, her parents had insisted that she marry before her child was born.

Each woman had her own opinions about the Party, the social and political system in the GDR, and the legal policies of the new unified German government. Some of the most critical voices came from women who left the Socialist Unity Party, the SED, while other criticisms were expressed by those who chose to retain their membership in the party that succeeded the SED after the *Wende,* the Party of Democratic Socialism, or PDS. Women with other party affiliations and those who proudly claimed no affiliation stated their political views as well. One interviewee deliberately avoided the term "we" in reference to the GDR and declared that she did not mourn its passing. Other women who had identified closely with the GDR had difficulty adjusting to the loss of their citizenship and culture.

Even when one tries to convey her experience accurately and objectively, personal accounts are inevitably affected by the process of remembering and narrating. Past events cannot be recalled completely, and each observer has a different perspective in assigning significance to a given occasion. Thus interviewees select and order the events in a unique way when relating a story. Moreover, the contradictions that sometimes appear within a single interview may result from an interviewee's desire to present herself as she wants to be perceived. Some East German women feel the need to justify their level of participation in the former system, knowing that a Western audience cannot comprehend the kind of conformity that is demanded in an authoritarian state. This collection of personal accounts does indeed consist of true stories, but they are "true" only insofar as personal narrative can ever be accurate.

With a selected bibliography and a glossary to elucidate terminology of the GDR, this book is a historically contextualized document that shows women taking advantage of new opportunities for public voice and involving themselves in shaping their new society. As Eva Kunz, Commissioner for Equal Opportunity in the East Berlin *Magistrat,* said about GDR women since the *Wende:* "Now women have found contact with the women's movement where they can learn to fight for what they want, which is tremendously important. . . . I have the impression that we are now coming back into history."

III

Since the *Wende,* many academics and political activists in East and West have pointed to the losses suffered by women in the process of German unification. One of numerous such voices, *Bundestag* representative Christine Schenck (Greens/Coalition 90) declared the proposed unification treaty to be a massive attack on the rights of women (*tageszeitung* 31.8.90, p.1). The imposition of the West German legal structure in the new federal states, for example, did away with a number of the progressive social policies for women. It has been argued in the growing body of scholarship on women in the GDR after unification that some East German women have also experienced significant economic setbacks in the new system.

At the time the original set of interviews was conducted just after unification, the notion of "women as losers" already permeated the German press. However, when interviewees were asked to comment on their own losses since the *Wende,* reactions were unpredictably varied. Almost all of the interviewees talked about a sense of gain as well as a sense of loss. To understand their responses, it is important to look at policy affecting East German women before the *Wende* in relationship to the changes that came with unification.

The unification treaty provided for the accession of the German Democratic Republic to the Federal Republic of Germany. What resulted in legal as well as practical terms was not the unification of two sovereign states; rather the legal system of the former FRG was applied, with few exceptions, to what had been the GDR—the economically weaker state. The unified country took not only the constitution of the FRG but also its name. Thus West German policy became effective for all of Germany.

Although most things changed for the GDR with the new constitution, one policy that remained the same was the codification of gender equality. The constitution of the German Democratic Republic had also guaranteed the equality of men and women and established a number of policies to secure statutory equality. One of the ways the socialist state attempted to achieve gender equality was through equal access to educational and professional opportunities. Although such factors as political record, family background and region of residence restricted equal access to education in the GDR, an increasingly larger percentage of women through the years completed educational programs. In the 1950s, only 5 percent of working women had participated in occupational or professional training. During the 1970s, that figure climbed to 60 percent of working women, and in 1988 reached 87 percent (Röth 134). By 1980, women had achieved almost 50 percent of the total university enrollments in the GDR, while women in the FRG had not yet reached 40 percent (Mushaben 5).

Although these figures suggest a genuine intent on the part of the SED state to provide equal education for women, some of the interviews contained here make clear that this commitment was only partial. For both male and female, choice of trade or profession was contingent upon availability of the desired study or training opportunity because entrance into professional and occupational tracks was centrally regulated. According to university student Marianne S., men were nonetheless more likely than women to be given their first choice. She said that despite the claim to equal access, men with lower grades than their female peers were still given preference in entering apprenticeships.

In the assignment of training programs, women were often steered away from higher paying occupations, which resulted in a gender classification of entire trades. In the 1980s, for example, 60 percent of the female apprentices were directed into ten "typically female"—and lower paying—job categories (Mushaben 6). Filmmaker Gitta Nickel, herself in a traditionally male field, confirmed in her interview that only a small number of women succeeded in making their way into male careers. In a gender-neutral occupation, however, women with the same qualifications as men were often assigned to lesser tasks and thus received lower pay (Rosenberg 138–39). Even with this apparent gender division of labor, women were integrated to some degree into the higher paying professions, yet men remained absent from traditionally female occupations (Nickel 48–49). An example can be seen in day care where, according to interviewee Eva Kunz, employees were exclusively women until just before the *Wende*.

The tendency to keep salary levels lower for the jobs traditionally held by women accounted for the fact that the average income for women in the GDR was about one-quarter less than for men. Another indicator of women's lower level earnings was the inequity in pensions. Political scientist Joyce Mushaben reveals that in 1989, only 131 men in the GDR received the absolute minimum pension of East Marks 330, in contrast to 103,000 women. The next level, East Marks 340, was paid to 423 men compared to 63,000 women (5). Germanist Eva Kolinsky states that because GDR women received lower pensions than men, they often were faced with poverty in their old age, despite a lifetime of paid work (278).

Construction worker Petra P. suggests in her interview that women who did work in traditionally male fields were sometimes looked upon as token females. As a middle manager, she herself was promoted and awarded prizes because she was the token woman. She also recalled a female colleague who said: "A woman manager is always talked about, regardless of whether she wears a short skirt or a long skirt, whether she wears flats or high heels, whether she wears make-up or no make-up, whether she takes a lot of sick leave or no sick leave. A man stays in a managerial position until it's been proven that he's not a manager, whereas a woman is not considered a manager until it is proven that she is one." In spite of gains made in access to traditionally male professions, the levels of advancement available to women were limited. The proportion of female academics and managers never transcended the 15 percent threshold at the highest levels (Mushaben 5). According to one interviewee, television film editor Gerda Maron, a management position in the GDR was out of the question for women with young children: "A big boss always has somebody at home doing the household chores and taking care of the children." Of the available management positions in the GDR, 35 percent were reported in the GDR press to have been occupied by women in 1989, but most of them were concentrated at lower or middle levels and in local rather than central administration (Mushaben 6).

The field in the GDR where women had least access was government. No woman ever sat in the SED's *Politbüro,* the highest governing body. In the forty years of the GDR, only five women held the post of minister, and none of them ever belonged to the Presidium of the Council of Ministers (Mushaben 7). The situation of proportional representation in government improved for women at the lower end of the hierarchy. Of the five hundred representatives in the GDR's Peoples Chamber (*Volkskammer*), almost one-third were women in 1982 (*Panorama* 1983, 58). In the early 1980s approximately one-fourth of the city mayors were women, although all of the major cities were administered by men. The responsibilities of local administrators often included implementing by fixed procedures the official policy that had been previously decided by men on a higher rung of the hierarchical ladder. According to interviewee Eva Kunz: "On the local level we had women mayors, and women sat on district councils, but those activities were not political. People in those positions simply confirmed decisions that had already been made; politics occurred elsewhere."

Comments from the interviewees also call into question the claim of East German women's equal access to educational and professional opportunities. One strong voice on the subject was middle-manager Petra P., who claimed: "The promotion of women was just something that was printed on paper."

Katharina Stillisch, press secretary for the Commissioner for Equal Opportunity, was of the same opinion: "Men don't want women in leading positions—and certainly not capable women—because they are afraid of such women." Germanist Dorothy Rosenberg argues that the level of female participation in economic and political spheres was affected by women's continued responsibility for family. In addition, society devalued "female" qualities such as creativity, nurturing, and emotional sensitivity, as well as "female" roles such as teaching and caregiving (141). Eva Kunz concurred: "What is astounding is that women's economic independence didn't affect the traditional understanding of gender roles."

A major shift in the promotion of women to positions of responsibility can be noted in the brief period of greater self-determination between the fall of the Honecker government and German unification. During this time, a high percentage of elected administrative positions in educational institutions were filled by women. This change reflected the move for democratic reform that was inspired by the oppositional movements and the direct democracy of the "Round Table," an unofficial, multiconstituency advisory body to the interim government of Hans Modrow, which lasted from November 1989 until the *Volkskammer* elections in March 1990. Another sign of the efforts made for a more equal representation was the granting of four highly visible government posts to women during this period (Rosenberg 142). Since unification, the number of women leading ministries at the state level has increased significantly in both the new federal states and the old ("Week in Germany" 6–7).

To understand why the GDR promoted the education of women, it is important to remember its beginnings. In the early years of postwar reconstruction, between 1945 and 1953, the state found itself in a double bind, needing reproduction as much as it needed production. The developing economy had to have women in the work force, and it also needed offspring for future workers. By 1972 the state had established policies that strongly encouraged women to pursue the dual role of full-time worker and mother.

The most notable of these supports for the working mother was the "baby year." For the first child, a mother received twenty-six weeks of maternity leave on full pay. Women with more than one child could extend that leave to a full year, the so-called *Baby-Jahr* (Kolinsky 264). The social policy after unification provides only eight weeks of automatic postpartum leave (Mushaben 5). In addition, mothers in the GDR could stay home with their babies for two more years at a percentage reduction of their salary. They had a guarantee of return to their previous job or one with corresponding pay. Although most mothers returned to work immediately after the paid leave of absence, some chose to stay home longer than the allotted maternity leave "to accompany their children's development," as public administrator Eva Stahl described it. If a parent wanted to stay home without pay beyond three years, reentry into the work force was still possible at any time because of the guaranteed right to work in the GDR. Even though staying home with children for longer periods was possible, it was not very common because the state encouraged return to the work force.

The availability of inexpensive child care also aided mothers in combining work and family. Single mothers depended upon this service, and one-third of first-time mothers in the GDR were single. Of all East German children under three years old, 84 percent attended *Kinderkrippe,* and 90 percent of those between three and five attended *Kindergarten* (equivalent to "day care" in the United States and will be referred to here as such). Because night work for women was not against the law in the GDR, many of the state-supported child care facilities took care of children on an overnight basis (Mushaben 5). Katharina Stillisch and environmentalist Maria Curter admitted that they would not have chosen to have children without the availability of day care.

Although many appreciated the advantages of day care, some mothers criticized the quality of care given. Others argued that taking a small baby away from the primary care-giver had negative psychological consequences. Parents complained about overcrowding, the rigidity of the daily routine, the attempt to control the children's emotional responses, the heavy ideological content of the centrally designed program, and the ratio of care-giver to child—between 1 to 15 and 1 to 20 (Maaz 25–31). Physical therapist Karin Tittmann told of campaigning with other mothers for the removal of army tanks from the day care toy collection: "We discussed it over and over at school, and finally we just went into the classroom, opened the closet and took out the tanks. We said: 'If you keep the tanks we'll take our children home.'" Not all shared this critical view, however. Eva Stahl said that the quality of care depended to a great degree on the staff of a particular facility. She asserted that some attendants were remarkably creative and caring, providing children with a nurturing environment that was healthier than what they would have known in homes where the parents were constantly overworked.

After unification many day care facilities were closed because of insufficient funding. Even before unification, the moribund East German economy had difficulty maintaining its day care subsidies. Economically dysfunctional factories could not support day care facilities any more than they could continue to pay the salaries of superfluous employees. Still, the noticeable reduction in inexpensive day care has been one of the widely regretted losses since the *Wende*.

Unsubsidized day care in the new system is considered to be inordinately expensive for many East German women who do not yet earn salaries that correspond to the West German pay scale. Indeed costs for day care in West Germany in 1989 ranged from DM 250 to DM 1500 per month, compared to roughly East Marks 30 to 50 in the GDR (Mushaben 5). Interviewee Marianne S. said that since unification, students at the Humboldt University in Berlin have found a way around these high fees by establishing a cooperative day care program where parents provide care themselves on a rotating basis.

Another benefit intended to promote the dual responsibility of career and children in the GDR was the "household day," one working day off per month granted to all married women, to single women with children under sixteen, and to women without children who had reached the age of forty (*Panorama* 1987, 12). Petra P. said that she misses the household day, although she admitted that the increase in paid vacation days at her new job makes up for the loss. Eva Stahl claimed that the household day was sometimes used as an excuse for bosses not to give other breaks that mothers sometimes needed, such as more flexible working hours to get the children to day care. Although working women appreciated the household day, they still worked two days per month more than people in the FRG, where the work week was roughly six hours less than in the GDR.

The household day was a gesture that recognized the additional burden of domestic responsibilities for working women, but it also reinforced the gender division of labor, relegating household chores to the domain of women. Although the privilege of the household day could have been taken also by fathers, men seldom took advantage of it. Maria Curter suggested that for a significant part of the population, it was socially unacceptable for a man to care for either the household or the children. Men who considered taking the household day, according to Curter, were told by their peers to "get a girlfriend." The implication was that domestic duties need not be shared. Married women without children were granted the household day—apparently expected to take care of their husbands—but single women without children were not (until they reached the age of forty).

Another bonus was twenty to twenty-three days annual paid time-off (at 90 percent of salary) to care for a sick child. This was granted to all single mothers and to married mothers with at least two children, according to a sliding scale that benefited women with more than one child: twenty-three days for mothers with three children under sixteen, twenty-two days for mothers with two children, and so on (Winkler *Frauenreport* 81). In 1989 this leave accounted for an average of 1.5 million work days per month (Winkler *Frauenreport* 82). Interviewee Eva Peter complained that this time to care for sick children was widely misused because young mothers often took more than the necessary leave. Physician Haiderun Lindner expressed the same idea a bit differently: "If a department had eight people and four of them were young women with children, and two of those positions were empty because children were sick, then the whole department was maintained by the fifty-year-old women with this strong sense of responsibility. . . . We often said that our entire economy was being supported by fifty-year-old women with varicose veins." Since unification this paid leave amounts to only five days per year.

Other benefits to ease the financial burden of raising children included a monthly subsidy for each child. In 1987 the amount was East Marks 50 per child for up to three children (Kolinsky 263). The sum was similar in the FRG. In 1992 a new law established that this subsidy would vary according to income. The GDR paid a "birth benefit" to all women in the amount of East Marks 1000, more than the average woman's monthly salary. The birth benefit in the West amounted to only DM 150, about one-twentieth of the average salary. To encourage marriages, GDR couples received a "marriage benefit," a special interest-free loan of East Marks 5000, which was raised to 7000 in 1989. Up to Marks 5000 of this loan could be progressively cancelled according to the number of children one bore: 1000 for the first child, 1500 for the second, and 2500 for the third (*Panorama* 1987, 22). Because this loan was only available to people under twenty-five (in 1989 the age limit was raised to thirty), it might have prompted the large number of young marriages in the GDR (Mushaben 5). The "marriage benefit" as such does not exist in the new Germany, but financial breaks are given to married heterosexual couples in other ways, from income-tax reductions to state-subsidized loans for purchasing or building a home.

IV

While the postunification changes affected women in a variety of ways, none was as troubling as the loss of job security. In socialist Germany the right to gainful employment was guaranteed in the constitution, which meant that women with or without children could depend on a regular income. Although the choice of fields might be limited, a job of some kind was guaranteed. The importance of employment to East German women is reflected in the centrality of the topic in the interviews. A number of women said that work contributed to their self-esteem. "I couldn't imagine life without work," Katharina Stillisch reported. Writer Helga Schütz said that this was a common perspective: "All around me here are women who worked because they wanted to and wouldn't have given it up." Even though some of the interviewees expressed dissatisfaction with certain aspects of their work, all treasured the right to gainful employment—whether its primary advantage was financial independence from a man, an avenue for self-expression, a place for participation in a community of women, or simply an escape from boredom.

It is not surprising that paid work was so highly valued in a society that supported the Marxist notion of "non-alienating work." The print media in socialist Germany testified to the high priority given to the concepts of "work" and "workers," and the government proclaimed itself a "Nation of Workers and Peasants" (*Arbeiter-und Bauernstaat*), the GDR's equivalent to the American "Land of the Free." Because work was also considered a duty, virtually all women were expected to work for most of their adult lives. Throughout the 1980s, 91 percent of East German women between the ages of eighteen and sixty were either gainfully employed or in training (Rosenberg 138).

By July 1992, however, almost one-fourth of the GDR labor force was technically unemployed, and slightly over half of that figure were women (Winkler *Sozialreport* 78). Those hit particularly hard by the wave of terminations were women over forty, who often faced age-discrimination in seeking reemployment, and single mothers who saw unemployment as a threat to their existence. Even some who were not directly affected by lay-offs worried about the repercussions of the widespread unemployment.

A number of women, however, were less pessimistic about the new problem of unemployment. Eva Stahl said that she welcomed temporary unemployment as a reprieve from the unrelenting stress of the double burden of family and work. She was grateful for the unemployment compensation she drew for a brief period because no such support had existed in the GDR. By contrast, after six months on unemployment compensation, Katharina Stillisch preferred the subsidized employment in the GDR over unemployment compensation in the FRG. In her view, people had a greater sense of self-respect when the government created a job for them than when it handed them a check. Ursula Korth, who worked in film purchasing for East German television, concurred: "The most important thing is to keep my job. I can't imagine living on welfare or unemployment compensation."

Some women who did not have to make a choice between work and family in the previous system felt that they are being forced to do so by the new system. The decreased financial support for managing both work and family and the loss of self-respect that accompanied economic autonomy are seen as significant setbacks for many women in the new federal states. For those who defined themselves to a large degree through their work, unemployment requires an enormous psychological reorientation and, in some cases, a significant economic adjustment. Some East German women, however, are celebrating the shift to a social market economy. Still others find it painful to recognize with the switch to a market economy that the roots of the rampant unemployment following unification could be traced back to, among other things, many years of economically inefficient employment practices in their own country. Petra P. reinforced this thought in reference to those who "enjoyed privileges and ruined the economy": "If our industry hadn't been in such terrible shape we could have prevented a lot of the present unemployment because the factories would still be functioning." A small chemical plant in Saxony, one of many such examples, had employed forty-nine workers when only six were needed (Prausa 10).

When the first interviews were conducted in late 1990 and early 1991, roughly half of the women worried about losing their jobs. By the second round of interviews in July 1992, many had shifted to new jobs—an indication of the volatility of the postunification employment situation. A brief look at changes in the employment status in this period shows how the interviewees had adjusted in the new system. Two of the women could not be reached for a second interview. Of the remaining sixteen, none was without a regular income, although some were concerned that they might yet become unemployed.

Five women reported in the first interview that they would be laid off when the organizations they worked for were dismantled (the East German television network, the DEFA film studio, and the East Berlin *Magistrat*). However, all were again employed: two in West German firms, and two working with women's issues in government. Only the fifth was dissatisfied with her new position because she felt that she was working far below her qualifications.

Five of the women had lost their permanent jobs but had signed other contracts, three of which were "ABM" positions (*Arbeitsbeschaffungsmaßnahmen*), jobs created by the government that generally lasted two years. One woman with temporary employment had become the program director of a center that helped reintegrate women into the work force. She hoped that the center would be financially self-sufficient by the time the government support expired.

One interviewee was paid a salary-stipend while taking part in a retraining program of her choosing. Another was guaranteed a job for only one more year, at which time she might be rehired into the newly privatized firm. Four other women had become self-employed. Of the original twenty-six interviewees, only one was unemployed in the summer of 1992: a published writer who was drawing a year of unemployment compensation.

Although one cannot come to conclusions on the basis of such a small sampling of predominantly educated women, the second set of interviews suggests a shift in attitudes. The frustration and fear evident in the first conversations had receded for some women. The barrage of tax and insurance forms had been filled out and sent in. All had traveled to the West, whether to West Berlin, Sweden, Canada, or England. Although rents and utility bills were still rising, some women seemed better able to deal with the economic uncertainty than they had been immediately following unification. Two of the women with temporary positions stated that they had never earned as much money—nor worked as hard. Both liked their jobs and hoped that they would become permanent. Although some women were not happy with their changed situation, others showed an emerging optimism. One woman was excited that, in her new job, hard work was recognized and rewarded. A self-employed woman felt proud of her thriving business. Others had similar stories. In general, the second set of interviews indicates a shift toward greater hope and a sense of more control over a still uncertain but increasingly familiar environment.

V

Many of those interviewed indicated that because paid employment had meant economic independence for East German women, they believed the guarantee of a job had brought them some measure of equality with men. Many have argued, however, that neither equal opportunity nor equal status really existed in the GDR (see Kuhrig and Speigner, Böhme, Friedrich-Ebert-Stiftung). According to Parliament member Jutta Braband: "Even with the same education or training as men, even with salaries that were almost the same as men's . . . , all of this didn't add up to equality." She emphasized that as important as codified legal equality is, it alone is not enough: "While women in the West were fighting for equal rights, we wanted equal status because we knew from experience that having equal rights isn't enough. Real equal opportunity is what's important, not the fact that some law states that I have equal rights. If in reality the man is always preferred over me, then I don't have a chance."

Katharina Stillisch explained that what the state offered women should more accurately be called a *Scheinemanzipation* (false emancipation) because the traditional attitudes toward keeping woman in her place—second place—lay just below the surface. She continued: "Women had equal rights, but they didn't have equal rights. . . . Women and men are *not* equal. There are still some who are a little more equal, and those are the men." GDR-generated material sometimes cautiously admitted the same. For instance, a public relations booklet that described the country's special programs for women stated: "Old, outdated ideas according to which women are housewives above all have not completely died out in socialism" (*Panorama* 1983, 59).

In an unconventional stance on women's policy in socialist Germany, East German social scientist Irene Dölling asserted that the benefits for women in the GDR were not necessarily woman-friendly. Rather they were measures to maintain the patriarchal hierarchy at many levels of society by creating women's dependency—not on a husband—but on the generous hand of "father-state" (125–33). Females in the GDR were not to grow up. This dependency—economic and psychological—was evident in all aspects of society beginning with the earliest years of day care. Taking issue with the commonly held view that these policies promoted women, Dölling argues that they in fact sustained the patriarchal status quo by exploiting women as cheap labor and baby bearers (127, 130).

Other criticisms raised against the "mommie-policies" (*Muttipolitik*) argue that working mothers were adversely affected because they had to master at least two full-time responsibilities with no time left for themselves. As urban planner Tina F. noted: "The emphasis on work and family [in the GDR] never allowed women time for self-examination." Some also agreed with Dölling that the promotion of the working mother was detrimental to women in general because it ignored the diversity of women, overlooking their various needs and interests (123, 131). If women without children were generally valued less, lesbians were completely ignored. Lifeguard Heike Prochazka said: "I had never

heard of homosexuality. . . . It wasn't talked about." Deliberate lack of acknowledgment of women who did not fit the image of the working mother reinforced
traditional attitudes toward homosexuality.

Despite the heavy criticisms of the state's approach to securing gender equality, however, many women claimed to have achieved an inner emancipation.
Helga Schütz stated: "Women here were emancipated, but it was tremendously
difficult for them because they had to fight for their everyday existence. . . . You
can't see their emancipation on the outside. But you can see on the inside that
they have worked, that they are independent, and that they know life." Journal
editor Ursula Sydow remarked: "I think women in the GDR had a lot of self-
confidence. . . . Some men had a hard time dealing with these self-confident
women because they were absolutely independent." The self-respect acquired
through active participation in the work force nurtured for some the kind of
assertiveness and independence that contribute to a personal emancipation.

Even though many women valued this inner emancipation acquired on their
own and the economic independence provided by the GDR state, they resented
the lack of self-determination that permeated other areas of their lives, such as
the inability to travel at will, to live in the apartment of their choosing, to
practice various forms of spirituality, or to organize a public feminist reading
circle. In the words of Maria Curter: "The state took a lot off your shoulders,
but it demanded something in return: the right to tell you what to do." Eva
Kunz concurred: "Women in the GDR were not emancipated in the sense that is
understood in the West. But then the men weren't either." Declaring that emancipation means more than economic independence, Kunz continued: "It means
that a woman can determine for herself her place in society, and that didn't
happen here."

VI

The sense of loss and anxiety that persists in the new federal states—even when
accompanied by appreciation for the gains that have come with unification—
will likely not disappear before the end of the century. It derives from more
than simply the loss of job security; it is inseparable from the loss of autonomy,
of history, and of identity. Attempts to ignore or play down this very deep loss
only exacerbate the difficulties of east-west dialogue. Likewise, overlooking the
losses particular to women perpetuates the age-old problem of silencing them.
Emphasizing what has been taken from women relegates them to the unpro-

ductive role of objects of history and discourages them from becoming historical actors themselves.

Accepting setbacks for women as historically justified reinforces the belief that women are inferior. In this respect, the plight of women in the aftermath of the *Wende* is nothing new. Unfortunately, however, attention to the topic of women in the process of German unification has concentrated almost exclusively on what they lost with little mention of the positive aspects of the transition. This emphasis on loss—like a self-fulfilling prophecy—ironically affirms it. Those women who make the transition work for them feel silenced by the message that "women are the losers of German unification." Some feel guilty about their personal and professional successes. Women who make contributions in the new society are many, but their stories are given little attention.

It becomes clear when reading through the compiled interviews that the perception of women as losers has to be reexamined. These women have been actively involved in re-creating their new environment. In the words of retired professor and women's activist Hanna Behrend: "After the collapse of the old system in October 1989, things happened terribly quickly, and one of the things that happened was that women began to organize themselves in a way they had never done before." Giving a number of examples, Katharina Stillisch asserted: "Women's projects have sprung up everywhere since the *Wende*." Even though most of the women regret or resent many of the changes brought by the new system, they are finding ways to take responsibility for their own lives through initiative, diligence, and creativity. They are active participants in the new society rather than passive victims of a patriarchal state. Their stories suggest that economic autonomy was not the only kind of independence that East German women possessed. The women interviewed, and many like them in the new Germany, are successfully negotiating the obstacles of this transition by demonstrating the resourcefulness and integrity that have constituted women's strength for centuries.

Works Cited

Böhme, Irene. "Die Frau und der Sozialismus." *Die da drüben.* Berlin: Rotbuch, 1983. 82–
        107.
Chronik der Ereignisse in der DDR. *Deutschland Archiv.* Köln: Verlag Wissenschaft und
        Politik, 1989.
Die DDR *stellt sich vor.* Berlin: Panorama DDR, 1986.
Dölling, Irene. "Alte und neue Dilemmata: Frauen in der ehemaligen DDR." *Women in*

German Yearbook 7. Ed. Jeanette Clausen and Sara Friedrichsmeyer. Lincoln: University of Nebraska Press, 1991. 121–36.

Friedrich-Ebert-Stiftung, ed. *Frauen in der* DDR. *Auf dem Weg zur Gleichberechtigung?* Bonn: Verlag Neue Gesellschaft, 1987.

Holschuh, Albrecht. "Protokollsammlungen der DDR." *German Studies Review* 15.2 (May 1992): 267–87.

Kirsch, Sarah. *Die Pantherfrau: Fünf unfrisierte Erzählungen aus dem Kassetten-Recorder.* Berlin and Weimar: Aufbau, 1973.

Kolinsky, Eva. *Women in Contemporary Germany: Life, Work, and Politics.* Providence, Oxford: Berg Publishers, 1993.

Kuhrig, Herta, and Wulfram Speigner, eds. *Wie emanzipiert sind die Frauen in der* DDR? Köln: Pahl-Rugenstein, 1979.

Maaz, Hans-Joachim. *Der Gefühlsstau. Ein Psychogramm der* DDR. Berlin: Argon, 1990.

Mushaben, Joyce. "Paying the Price of German Unification: Männer planen, Frauen baden aus," GDR *Bulletin* 17.2 (Fall 1991): 3–9.

Nickel, Hildegard M. "Sex-Role Socialization in Relationships as a Function of the Division of Labor: A Sociological Explanation for the Reproduction of Gender Differences." *The Quality of Life in the German Democratic Republic: Changes and Developments in a State Socialist Society.* Ed. Marilyn Rueschemeyer and Christine Lemke. Trans. Michel Vale. Armonk, NY: M.E. Sharpe, 1989: 48–58.

Panorama DDR-*Do You Know about the* GDR? Dresden: Grafischer Großbetrieb Völkerfreundschaft, 1983.

Panorama DDR-*Sozialpolitik.* Dresden: Grafischer Großbetrieb Völkerfreundschaft, 1987.

Prausa, Eva-Maria. "Reprivatization in the ex-GDR." Trans. Pam Allen. Unpublished manuscript of lecture given at Hamilton College, New York, March 1991.

Röth, Uta. "Die klassenlose Gretchenfrage. Über die Vereinbarkeit von Beruf und Familie." *Wir wollen mehr als ein Vaterland.* Ed. Gislinde Schwarz and Christine Zenner. Reinbek bei Hamburg: Rowohlt, 1990: 132–44.

Rosenberg, Dorothy. "Shock Therapy: GDR Women in Transition from a Socialist Welfare State to a Social Market Economy." *Signs* 17.1 (Autumn 1991): 129–51.

Wander, Maxie. *Guten Morgen, du Schöne.* Darmstadt: Luchterhand, 1979.

"The Week in Germany." German Information Center, New York. (1 May 1992): 6–7.

Winkler, Gunnar, ed. *Frauenreport '90.* Berlin: Verlag die Wirtschaft, 1990.

———. *Sozialreport '90: Daten und Fakten zur sozialen Lage in der* DDR. Berlin: Verlag die Wirtschaft, 1990.

Hanna Behrend,

sixty-eight, retired associate
professor of English,
Humboldt University

January 1991

I met Hanna Behrend at "Eva," a new women's center in Prenzlauer Berg where she was attending a meeting of women from the PDS, the Party of Democratic Socialism. Professional retirement had not curtailed her political activities. She appeared to be just as active at age sixty-eight as she had been at twenty-four when she moved from Austria to Soviet-occupied Berlin in 1946 to build a country that would be, as she called it, "a kind of beacon for the world."

Hanna Behrend was eager that her story be heard. She thought that news reports in the West had focused too heavily on the negative side of life in the GDR in an attempt to paint the Wende *as the victory of good (democracy) over evil (socialism). She declared, "Presenting a monolithic picture of what was going on here is all wrong." She wanted people outside the GDR to know that there had been good among the bad. However, she was not hesitant to look at the shortcomings of the SED-state, especially its treatment of women. She decried the paternalistic character of the old system which purported to emancipate women by making it easier for them to have both family and profession but, in fact, kept men and women firmly within the framework of traditional gender roles. As an early member of the Autonomous Women's Association, she shared with other feminists the desire to replace the patriarchal system with a truly egalitarian system where women would have a greater measure of self-determination, and both men and women would share equal responsibility for the care of children.*

She further criticized the SED by claiming: "The leadership was not socialist." At the same time, as a member of the Party rank and file she felt partially responsible for the failure of socialism in the GDR. "Why did we allow ourselves to be be-

trayed?" she asked. "A more productive question is why we didn't do anything about it."

After a six-year stay in England during World War II and years of teaching the English language, Hanna Behrend spoke fluent English. Thus this interview was conducted in English.

Hanna Behrend

During the *Wende,* after the collapse of the old system in October 1989, things happened terribly quickly, and one of the things that happened was that women began to organize themselves in a way they had never done before. Their first goal was to discuss what kind of society they really wanted. Their strongest reproach of the old system was its paternalistic character, the fact that whatever concerned women was not self-determined but rather had been decreed from above, and women had to take it or leave it. All the social advantages women had, as compared with women in Western countries, were not brought about by their own efforts: there was nothing they did politically as women. If they ever did anything it was within the structures that existed in the country, which left them very little option for self-determination.

After the October events women got together, and their first objective was to criticize the state of things. They didn't want the uniform type of day care facilities. They criticized the fact that women had been strongly discouraged from adopting any lifestyle other than traditional marriage, or if not marriage, heterosexual partnership. They concentrated on all the shortcomings that had been characteristic of the old system. But they had very little time to work all this out and even less time to change things. Before they could get down to changing anything, a second big political change came about. Women were still discussing all sorts of things, while in the factories, in the shops, and in academic institutes people were already being fired. Day care centers belonging to certain firms were closed or had to be taken over by the community. After the change in the political system, the second change had to do with the change of the actual social system, which the women only noticed rather late.

The reason why people went into the streets to topple the old government had little to do with what they have now got. They wanted a better society but they didn't want to get rid of whatever achievements they had gained. Despite all the negative features of the past system, it had certain features that were very much worth preserving. Nobody really wanted to do away with the right to work or cheap meals at school. Nobody really wanted to do away with the baby year. What they wanted was the baby year optional for either parent. The male partner could take the baby year but that rarely happened. There were a lot of other things that they would not have wanted to do without, had they thought about it.

The majority were not worried about politics. What they had always been worried about was that they couldn't buy all the things they wanted and that the situation of the consumer was so inferior to that of the West German consumer, which they knew about from their relatives. What they hated was that they could not travel freely. Those are totally justifiable concerns. But beyond that they took everything they had for granted. That is to say, whatever advantages they had compared with Western countries did not really seem advantages to them; they seemed something that wasn't worth talking about. From what they gathered, there was full employment in West Germany. There was indeed a very high rate of employment, that is perfectly true. And so they didn't think it was necessary to worry about a job.

This was the frame of mind of most people, and particularly women, because women were doing the bulk of the shopping. If women are constantly confronted with things that they can't get and find it difficult to provide their family with, then the matter of consumption is not one of plenty or prosperity, but it's a vital need. Therefore it's perfectly legitimate for these women to feel that a society that can't provide plenty, or at least a sufficiency of things, wasn't a society they wanted to defend.

As early as October 1989, the demonstrations that took place on Mondays changed in character. They stopped using the slogan "We are the people" and began to intonate "We are *one* people." This didn't come about by itself, although most of the politicians insist that this was the popular soul that suddenly expressed itself. What really happened is that huge masses of representatives from West German parties flooded into what was then the GDR, including quite a bunch of right wing extremists, and promised the world or "prosperity in our day." And this sounded quite reasonable because for years people had been indoctrinated by the various West German governments by means of television—and everyone except the poor people in Dresden could and did get Western stations—and much better indoctrinated than they ever were by the ghastly GDR media.

In December Helmut Kohl himself—the great Kohl—came to Dresden and promised the D-Mark and lots of other things. There was every reason for the ordinary person here to think that, if only there was unification, within weeks, within months, or certainly within a couple of years, the prosperity of the prosperous West Germans would have come to us. This was what the people thought who had been concerned about the lack of freedom to travel and the lack of consumer goods.

But I want to get back to the women. The women who formed the Autonomous Women's Association were very largely academic women. This isn't surprising; it's the same everywhere. It has so far not been possible for this new women's movement to really recruit women who are blue-collar or office workers. These latter women are on the whole suffering in silence. Quite a lot of them have lost their jobs, and some are becoming active in the trade union movements.

After this galloping consumption-oriented unification took place, particularly after July 1990 when the currency union was established, the complete smashing up of GDR industry occurred. What industries needed was investment so they could modernize their equipment. Industry was not entirely derelict. This is a myth. Quite a lot of industries were flourishing, for example the textile industry in Thuringia, and many were quite modern. But they were competed into oblivion. The same thing happened with the food industry. One example. We always used to buy a certain kind of low-fat butter which was low in calories but still tasted like butter, which margarine doesn't. Until recently I was still able to get it, but now it is completely gone. I'm now obliged to buy high-fat butter, which I don't want and my husband can't eat, or I have to go back to margarine, which I've loathed since World War II. I have no option. This so-called pluralistic society forces me to do something even in the realm of consumption which I don't want to do. I'm obliged right and left to take things as I find them, which is of course what I always used to have to do, but with all this talk about all the options that I have, I find that I don't have any, or I don't have any more than I had before.

What happened, instead of having improved facilities and quality of life, while we were still talking about how we were going to get this greater freedom of lifestyles and plurality, women were being fired at most of the firms. Academic women are in a particularly gruesome situation. That has to do with the complete smashing up of most of the academic institutions, particularly in the social sciences. The reproach is being made that all these social science academies were good for nothing but state propaganda, claimed by people who in most instances are not competent to judge and have not the slightest idea of what really did go on. Of course everything in a country that is subsidized is state-supporting. You can't be non–state-supporting if you get money from the state. But there was a considerable freedom of research and teaching. I have been a university teacher for almost thirty years. I have never had anyone snooping in my lectures, or sitting in my lectures and scribbling, or reporting me, or doing anything of the sort. Nobody has ever stopped me from teaching what I wanted to teach or even made me proclaim certain things that I did not believe in. I'm not saying that never happened to anyone. But I'm saying that there were enough options for the individual teacher that you could act in one way or you could act in another way. You were not forced for the sake of keeping your job to denounce people. You were not forced for the sake of not being thrown in jail to get up and lecture on the greater glory of Erich Honecker. At least, I was never asked to do anything of the sort, and I've taught at two universities, at the English language department of Humboldt University and at the closed-down College of Economics.

Presenting a monolithic picture of what was going on here is all wrong. It just wasn't true. It's no more true than in any other place in the world. There were teachers and officials, of course, who did persecute students who were opposed to the regime and who made their lives impossible and tried to remove them from the university, and were in many cases successful. But there were others who would never do anything of the sort.

The history of this GDR state has still to be written. It underwent quite different phases. It was never of one piece. It was always a process of great contradictions. After all is said and done, lots of the structures were not capitalist structures; they were noncompetitive. That meant that although this was a police state, and although a lot of awful things happened—unforgivable things which were definitely the root of the eventual collapse—it was also true that nobody was hungry, nobody was homeless, nobody was left to go to hell or to the next place.

I came here from Austria in 1946 because I thought there was great hope to change for the better, for something that would be a kind of beacon for the world, a country that had gone through a horrible history. I now feel in a way responsible for our not having achieved this aim. I can't yet say where we failed. I don't mean where this leadership failed, that's obvious enough, but where this SED rank and file failed. Many of the people who belonged to the rank and file were not in it just to get a job. A lot of people *were* in it just to get a job. But there were a lot of people—maybe they were a minority but they were a substantial minority—that had got in particularly when they were young students and workers because they wanted to change the world, to improve things, to take socialism at its word. You can say we were all betrayed, but you can also ask, why did we allow ourselves to be betrayed. A more productive question is, why didn't we do anything about it.

People are always asking me if I was privileged. I don't think so. It is true that certain leading jobs were staffed by people who were either Party members before they took the job or else were asked to take out a Party card in order to get the job. There were such jobs, particularly on the management level in industry. The top echelons of the university, such as the chancellor and vice-chancellors, were SED Party members. I don't know of any case where this was not so.

However, in the university departments this was completely different. There's this myth that people in the Party were generally privileged and people who were not in the Party were generally not privileged. In fact, the non-Party members had just as much authority and were just as much involved in decision making as the Party members. They were also directors of research and department heads (*Sektionsdirektor*), and so forth. The hierarchical structure and "leading role of the Party" meant, however, that the range of their decision making was relatively limited and subject to approval from above.

It is also being mythologized at the moment that the ordinary non-Party member was downtrodden, oppressed, and could never get anywhere. The people who were really threatened with *Berufsverbot*, which meant being banned from their profession, or who were threatened with imprisonment, were in most instances SED members, and later increasingly, people who were attached to the church. The people who were oppressed were people who really were political opponents, who were political people. The ordinary grouser who groused about there being no oranges in the shops was not oppressed.

I was a member of the SED and I was also member of the successor party, the PDS. But I turned in my Party card in January 1990 when they supported unification, after almost half a century of membership. Enough was enough. I'm as political a person as I always was, and the fact that I'm no longer a member of a political party hasn't changed that one iota. I still support all the things I supported before.

I've run feminist seminars for about five years. I haven't called them feminist, I've just done them. Actually in the last two years I've called them feminist theory, but before that I called them such things as Vera Brittain and the Peace Movement, Minor Writers, Modern English Literature. Since most of the students in this field are women, the group was almost always all women, with the occasional man. I've also had meetings once a month with women from all sorts of professions and walks of life and talked about women's problems.

I'm one of the very early members of the Autonomous Women's Association. At the moment there is a dwindling away of political activity among women. My impression is that people are completely inactive, or else they are stunned. Their attention is focused on losing their jobs and all the children's services, which I think is legitimate. From December 1989 to the monetary union in July 1990 the number of people interested in women's issues was growing. For the last half year at least, within the Women's Association I have had the feeling that there was a drying up, a declining, less activity. But there was nothing static about it.

I have a nightmarish feeling that the general political trend is to the right, to the dismantling of many of the things that were the result, particularly in West Germany, of the need to show that they were better than we were. This was one of the incentives for stabilizing what social services they have. You can't decline to do something if your neighboring German state has all these facilities. Maternity leave and other programs would never have been passed in West Germany without the social laws of the GDR.

At a demonstration against the Gulf War recently there was a woman who was carrying a poster saying something about Paragraph 218, and I heard somebody near me say, "That's out of place. What is she carrying that poster for?" And I had an argument with that one and said, "There's a definite connection." There's a lot of living life being killed now and at the same time they're making this fuss about pre-born life. I think all issues are connected. Women are losers on all sides.

July 1992

For Hanna Behrend the most significant change that had occurred since our first meeting was the decrease in women's financial security. More than half of the working women in the new federal states had lost their jobs, and the employment situation was worsening. "A minority of women in the women's movement think their world is sound, but for the vast majority the bottom has fallen out." New opportunities such as freedom to travel or to start a new business did not make up for the losses, she added. "Women are still the losers."

This insecurity had also made its way into her own life: her university pension, which had not been raised in three years, was scheduled to be cut. She had started legal proceedings against this cut, not entirely for the money—she also drew a "victim of fascism pension," a monthly sum paid by the government to those persecuted by the Nazis. Rather she wanted to make a political statement protesting this injustice. She said a number of former Humboldt faculty were doing the same thing.

In response to the question of what she missed about the GDR, she replied, "I miss the month after the demise of the GDR. I mourn the death of the potential." She added, however, that she did not miss the old system. She had known since the 1960s that it could not survive. When asked for an explanation, she responded, "A system that is so hierarchical, that coerces people, that gives them so little option of lifestyle, and that is based on the power privileges of a small minority, has to go. The problem is," she continued, "that the new system has many of the disadvantages of the old without its advantages."

As a postscript she added that although the negative trends described in her interview had increased, "the paralysis of the mind, the feeling of complete and utter powerlessness, of just having to swallow about everything, has come to a stop among increasing numbers of people. They are beginning to awaken and resist. What will become of this new awareness, already frightening the establishment, no one can tell. It may fade away, throttled by divisiveness—or it may rise, a new, wiser civil rights movement than the one before it."

Petra P.,

thirty-eight, formerly middle-manager in construction, now sauna attendant at a public swimming pool

March 1991

To many West Germans, Ossis (people from the East) were backward, lazy, and colorless. What emerges from Petra P.'s story, however, shows the folly of stereotyping. A strong woman, she refused to join the Party or to acquiesce to a system which she said promoted privilege in society and inequalities at work. She was able to achieve a high degree of independence both personally and professionally before the opening of the border and was taking advantage of the opportunities created since the Wende. *She tells of a post-*Wende *trip to visit a cousin in Schleswig-Holstein where she set foot on a golf course for the first time. She was surprised at how "normal" the "wealthy people" playing golf seemed to be. Similarly, the friends of her cousin were shocked when they discovered she was from East Berlin— so badly did she fit the stereotype of the meek* Ossi.

Work was important to her. She was promoted to the position of middle manager in a traditionally male area—construction. Even at that level, she was not taken seriously because she was a woman. "A man stays in a managerial position until it's been proven that he's not a manager, whereas a woman is not considered a manager until she has proven that she is one."

Although Petra P. chose to stay home with her small children, she resented the tedium of child-tending and the isolation she experienced in the "apartment city of Marzahn." She acknowledged the state's promotion of women with children but decried the lack of flexibility in working hours for women.

Petra P. was optimistic about the future. With the demise of the system which she said had prevented her from developing her full capabilities, she was now ready to take up the gauntlet thrown down by the West and was making the necessary arrangements to open her own fitness center.

Petra P.

I completed a training program in construction, and because I was the only female apprentice in the group, I had to learn to assert myself on the construction site and started becoming more self-confident. While I was going to college here in Berlin, I had to get married because I was pregnant. Pregnant women didn't really have to get married, but my parents wanted me to. They didn't want the marriage in the first place, but I wanted to get out of the house any way I could, so I left home and got an apartment with the help of the people at work. It was a three-room apartment, but one of the rooms was uninhabitable because the walls were completely wet. My husband had gone into the military for three years, and I hardly got any support from him. So I was alone in the apartment and had to deal with all sorts of situations by myself. I was constantly at odds with officials and had to pay a lot of fines. It was a time when I gained a sense of who I was, but I had to fight my way through.

My first husband's alcoholism played a decisive role in my decision to get out of the marriage. After my divorce, I got a job building new apartments and met my present husband. Then I started working at a training school where I organized educational programs for construction engineers. I was promoted to manager of a department with fifteen people under me.

I never had the feeling that I had to leave the GDR. However, I also have to say that as a department manager, I recognized the limits of our economy. I saw how much swindling went on, how the privileges that managers enjoyed were used, how certain people could decide who got what. That was tremendously frustrating for me. I was always coming into conflict with other managers because I'm very open and honest and tried to get things done by laying everything out on the table, by working together with others. But when I noticed that I wasn't being acknowledged I would get nasty. I was always having problems, so I thought about going to work for myself. I became serious about this in May 1989, before the *Wende,* and I said to myself, I can't stand this any more.

For example, in my position I was expected to discipline the people under me. First I had to clear the punishment with my superior, then I talked with the employee who might be reprimanded or warned. But this was terribly unpleasant, so people tried to sweep it under the carpet. In addition, my people knew that my boss and his friends took private trips and did other things during work time, and when I tried to reprimand my employees for not working hard enough or drinking on the job, they turned around and said to me, "That guy does this, and the other guy does that, and you want to punish me?" I couldn't handle that. The injustice, the refusal to do decent work, the pretending things were different than they were, all this was a corner I felt driven into.

I had tremendous problems with the Party secretary who told me when I started working in management that even though I wasn't in the Party I could come to him for advice or support at any time. There was a problem with one of my employees, so I went to him for help. But instead of help, I got the opposite. He made things very difficult for me. I was completely exhausted and psychologically defeated after I talked with him. There were Party members who were honest workers, but there were countless others who just sat at their desks and used their power to play with people. I hated that. I accept Party members in general if they are honest and say, "This is what I believe." But I don't accept the ones who were simply in the Party in order to get privileges or more money or a higher position. I've known some real bastards and I said to myself, I never want to belong to the same group as that person.

All this is a result of the system we had here. I am really angry that the big Party and government officials aren't being punished. I hoped that after the Wende, in recognition of those of us who really worked hard every day, that those people would be punished who took our money, enjoyed privileges, ruined our economy. They never put any money into the factories, and they were the reason the construction materials were of low quality and the technology was out of date. Now these people are getting their property back, and there are only show trials going on, for example against Harry Tisch, in order to keep the public quiet, and that's not enough as far as I'm concerned. I expect much much more from the present government. If all this hadn't happened, if our industry hadn't been in such terrible shape, we could have prevented a lot of the present unemployment because the factories would still be functioning.

I began to work on realizing my dream of opening up my own sauna with a fitness center and a solarium. I started making contacts and getting myself trained, and on January 1, 1990, I went to work at the sauna at a public pool to get the experience I need to open up my own sauna. The only thing I'm waiting for now is a piece of real estate where I can build. At present I'm negotiating with a firm to see if I can run their sauna and expand it. I'd rather have my own place, but this would be cheaper and would let me start small.

I was aware of my position as a woman in this society. When I got my managerial job at the construction office I had it hard. My immediate superior had never thought he would have a woman in the position. And then I turned up. He drew a very negative picture of my job and tried to scare me off. In hindsight I realize that it was very difficult for him to accept that I was a strong woman. I experienced this actually fairly often. There were always a lot of men in my department and they always tried to test me. At the beginning when I took the job, a woman colleague who was also in middle management gave me something she had written. At the end of this piece it said, "A woman manager is always talked about, regardless of whether she wears a short skirt or a long skirt, whether she wears flat shoes or high heels, whether she wears make-up or no make-up, whether she takes a lot of sick leave or no sick leave. A man stays in a managerial position until it's been proven that he's not a manager, whereas a woman is not considered a manager until she has proven that she is one." That made a lot of sense to me.

I found this to be true time and again. During the negotiations and discussions I had to lead, I had the sense that it was hard for the men to get used to the idea that a woman was standing up there in front of them, talking and making decisions. The curious thing about it all is that after my boss realized that I was a hard worker, he recommended me as his successor. He was the economic director of the company; he was sixty-two and thinking about retirement. I would have had to join the Party, and I didn't want to. I told him that, and so the whole thing died. I wouldn't have been very good in that job anyway. It amounted to little more than playing with numbers. You reported production numbers to the higher-ups, and the numbers were changed to reflect what they wanted. The numbers didn't reflect reality. With my penchant for honesty and forthrightness, that job wasn't for me.

I only experienced the so-called state promotion of women once. It was during my training program in construction when they saw that I was good and wouldn't give up. They awarded me a prize of a trip to the coast where I stayed in the company's vacation home, and I got the Karl Liebknecht medal for an excellent final exam. I could tell they were using me because I was a female apprentice and they wanted to play that up. Otherwise I never was promoted as a woman. On the contrary, I had to fight for the chance to work shorter hours when my older son started school. And that didn't help much either. I did work less, but the time away from work was the time the others used to sit around drinking coffee. I used the time to be with my son and help him with his homework and do housework.

I sent my children to day care and nursery school. I feel guilty now about my older son because he started going to day care when he was only two months old. I was going to college then and needed the time to study. When my second son was born, my husband wanted me to stay home for three years. But I couldn't stand being at home, so I took him to day care when he was two and a half. I was very alone here in this apartment city of Marzahn. There was just me and the four walls, plus diaper washing, taking the children for a ride in the baby buggy, feeding them, putting them to bed. I had hardly any contact with other women because most of them were at work. Then I had a miscarriage and was pretty distraught, although I didn't really want the baby. Two children were enough for me. I think that a working mother who is happy with her own life will be better with her children than a woman who stays home because she feels she has to. I don't think that helps the children.

It was always important for me to get to work on time, so I had to get the kids to day care at a certain time. That was terrible. I had to be at work at 7:00, and so I would drag the boy out of bed and dress him, even though he was old enough to dress himself, but it was faster if I did it. They were always talking about how much they were doing for mothers with children, but when I had to race to nursery school with a child in tow and then race to catch the bus because the director would carry on if I was five minutes late, that was bad. It would have been better if they had said that a mother with small children can get to work between 7:00 and 8:00 and make up the time on another day. Sometimes when I came to work late it wasn't because I was lazy but because my son had wet his pants just before we left the apartment. My husband got angry at me for being too short-tempered so I got him to take my second son to day care so he could see how it felt when he wouldn't put on his shoes or when he spilled cocoa on his shirt at breakfast or when he walked too slowly. Although he is a very quiet, even-tempered type, my husband had the same experience, and then he stopped scolding me.

It's important to me that I can travel now. Last September I visited a cousin of my mother's in Schleswig-Holstein by myself. I really enjoyed the visit and drank in the wonderful feeling of freedom. My friends wanted to play golf, so I caddied for them—this was the first time in my life that I had set foot on a golf course—and got to know some very wealthy people who, contrary to all my expectations, seemed completely normal. At dinner one night I sat next to a man who asked me where I was from, and I said Berlin, and then he asked, where in Berlin, and I said, Marzahn, and he asked, where's Marzahn, and I said, near Lichtenberg, and he said, I'm not familiar with Lichtenberg, I only know the Zoo train station. Then my cousin said, Petra, for God's sake, tell the man where you're from. So I said, I'm from East Berlin. There was absolute silence at the table; everyone sat there with their mouths open. They couldn't believe that I was from East Germany. Of course they all composed themselves very fast and were very nice to me, but they couldn't imagine that someone from East Berlin would be so normal and would look so good and would be able to carry on a conversation with them. My cousin said, Petra, you have to understand that you are all very exotic to us up here on the North Sea.

I'm really happy that we have the West German deutsch Mark, in fact that is one of the most important aspects of unification for me. People who had West money were always treated better than we were, with our East German Marks. I even experienced that within my own family. My husband's parents had access to West money and were given special treatment, whether it was with presents, or in a hotel. I was very aware of the difference it made if you had West money. These things hurt me because my parents and I had worked hard to earn our money and we simply couldn't buy anything else. The fact that someone had access to West money and because of that got special treatment was intolerable to me. I didn't go to visit my relatives in the West until I had some West money myself because I didn't want to depend on others. Now if I can earn more and save more I'll be able to buy a different car and travel differently, and I'll be viewed differently.

On November 9 I saw the press conference on TV, but somehow I didn't get what Schabowski was saying, what it all meant, that the border was open, that people could cross the border and leave. One of my colleagues walked into work the next day with a West Berlin newspaper and said, "I was over there." No one knew how long the border would stay open, whether it would be a day or a few hours, so I gave my secretary the day off and told her to go over and have a look. I was very happy, but I was crying too because it was incomprehensible. Suddenly everything was changed and somehow resolved. People felt free. It was amazing. I called our union representative because I wanted to tell her that I thought the open border was wonderful. Her reaction was very reserved. She said, "Who knows what will happen?"

There were certainly skeptics, people who couldn't deal with the new situation, the stubborn Party members who hung onto their old ideas. I think they felt betrayed, or maybe they had to wait to see what the Party would tell them to say about it. But for the people on the streets it was wonderful. I was not in the Party. My fear is that more and more people will want the old GDR back. I hear this at the pool—people tell me about their fears. I'm a sort of buffer for them. But I'm actually a very optimistic person and except for this one thing, I see the *Wende* as something very positive.

Whatever I have achieved in my life I achieved because I fought for it myself, because of my strong will, because I worked for it. Sometimes this fight exhausted me. Maybe I overestimated myself, but I tried to find a path to follow in my life, where I said to myself, you want this and here's what you have to do to get it. But I never ran to someone and said, I'm a woman, now help me, give me this. That's a totally foreign concept to me. The promotion of women was just something that was printed on paper.

Despite all the unemployment, my opinion of unification is very positive. The fact that I still have a job certainly influences the way I see things, but I see the negative things too. We're going through some very hard times now, but I think once our economy is unified and strong, we will have a decisive role in Europe and the world and can help other countries. I think the unification was exactly right. In fact, I think they should have done it a lot sooner. I'm very optimistic about the future. I think that after this economic decline that we're going through now, in five years we'll be living much better than if that Honecker had continued his rule. I believe this very strongly, and no one can shake my optimism.

July 1992

*The contract for the fitness center was ready to be signed when Petra P. became ill. During her hospital stay she had second thoughts about what it would mean to be self-employed: no health insurance, no vacation time. With fitness centers springing up on every corner, she also knew that competition would be fierce. Because of her background in construction, she landed a job when she recovered at the Housing Department (*Wohnungsaufsichtsamt*) where, among other things, she inspected apartments slated for renovation. "I really really like to go to work," she said. She was aware that she could lose her job—only civil servants had employment for life—but she felt confident that, because of the respect accorded her by her colleagues, she could probably keep her job as long as she wanted. "I don't think there will ever again be the security we had in the GDR," she commented. "Now you have to get that on your own. In general, people have to work much harder, but that's good." What she did miss about the GDR, however, was the household day.*

Petra P. was still very positive about her life since the Wende. *She laughingly* said, "Don't worry, be happy." She explained that with this attitude she could accomplish much more than if she were always complaining. She was grateful that her children had had no problems adjusting to the changes. Her older son was happy in his apprenticeship in West Berlin, and her younger son liked the new school system and the teachers' changed attitudes. She had just returned from vacationing in Schleswig-Holstein where, this time, she learned to play golf.

Eva Kunz,

forty-two, commissioner for Equal
Opportunity, *Magistrat*

December 1990

*In November 1990 the first Women's Conference for Security and Cooperation in
Europe was held in Berlin. The Women's Conference, independent from the established Conference for Security and Cooperation in Europe, was designed to formu-
late a slate of issues considered important for women—issues which were ignored
by the official, male-dominated CSCE. Among the many delegates from eastern and
western Europe was Eva Kunz, City Commissioner for Equal Opportunity (Stadt-
rätin für Gleichstellung) in the East Berlin* Magistrat, *who spoke articulately and
forcefully about the situation of women in East Germany after the* Wende. *Following her presentation, I asked her for an interview.*

Eva Kunz was upbeat and particularly positive about the Wende, *an attitude
which she attributed to her political activity before and after the autumn of 1989.
When the Wall opened, she had become active in SPD party politics, and in March
1990 had been elected to the People's Chamber (Volkskammer) in the first free East
German elections. She maintained that people who had participated in the political events of the last year of the GDR were far more likely to embrace the changes
brought on by the* Wende *than those "who stood by and felt the stream of history
wash over them." Her presentation at the Women's Conference was followed a few
months later by an interview in* Der Spiegel *(March 18, 1991) in which she was
cited as one of the few feminist activists in the East.*

*Eva Kunz presented a realistic, differentiated image of East German women,
some of whom she thought would encounter significant difficulties while others
would be able to negotiate the change very well. She was a strong woman with
confidence in the future.*

Eva Kunz

In general I think that for women some things will change more radically than for men because a conservative *Wende,* and this was a conservative *Wende,* is more difficult for women—or at least for certain women. I don't think we should fool ourselves; some women will be able to ride this conservative change very well, for example, women who want to stay home now because they have husbands with a good salary. We need to be careful not to say that all women should act in a certain way. There is no such thing as THE women.

I think that for women a change is taking place which will determine the shape of their lives. Before, they had a tremendous degree of security through their own income which affected, for example, a decision to divorce or a decision to have children without being married, which many women did. And now women find themselves suddenly in a system of dependencies—dependency on a partner or dependency on social welfare—and that is of course an entirely new way of living. On the one hand, I think it will be a more negative way of living because of the loss of security. On the other hand, women will have new opportunities to make themselves independent or to come together with other women. Before, there were hardly any women's groups where women could talk and learn and act together. Now women have found contact with the women's movement where they can learn to fight for what they want, which is tremendously important.

There was no women's movement here like the one in the West. There were no movements at all. I have the impression that now we're coming back into history. We've lived under a bell jar and very far removed from everything. I notice in myself that things affect me much more strongly than before, whether it's the Gulf War or the unification of Europe. Before the *Wende* we lived as if we were on the moon.

I sometimes wonder whether there was such a thing as politics in this country, a politics in which people participated. In the sense in which politics is understood in the West, there was none. On the local level we had women mayors, and women sat on district councils, but those activities were not political. People in those positions simply confirmed decisions that had already been made; politics occurred elsewhere. Politics has to be learned here, like many other things. Someone said that we have suddenly been thrown back into childhood and have to learn basic things, such as how to fill out a tax form. But I think we'll learn very fast.

I started meeting with a private women's group in the early eighties. We met in women's apartments and also within the church. We concerned ourselves with feminism and discussed very critically the society here and the things that we didn't like, for example, the fact that child care was always a woman's job, that men took no part in it, and that in the final analysis this society had a very traditional understanding of the roles of men and women. Then there was the group, Women for Peace, which was very active within the church. The church was the place where opposition could be articulated. Bärbel Bohley and Ulrike Poppe were both heavily involved in that group. Women were also active in a kind of literary salon, especially in Berlin, where forbidden literature was read and discussed. There was also a lesbian movement in the eighties, but it was always plagued by problems. When recently a wreath was laid to honor the lesbians who were killed in the women's camp at Ravensbrück, a huge panic broke out among the Stasi. There were always individual activities among women, but they never created a change in consciousness because they weren't public.

On the seventh of each month our small group demonstrated, sometimes at Alexanderplatz, sometimes elsewhere. It was exciting to observe the reaction of the people. Of course the demonstrators were eventually removed by the police or the Stasi, and even the people who walked by told us that we should go back to work instead of demonstrating. They disapproved of people who were saying that they saw things differently from what was printed in *Neues Deutschland,* the officially sanctioned newspaper.

That all changed on October 7 when suddenly people participated fully. I immediately joined the SPD and was elected to various positions, first to the Berlin SPD steering committee (*Bezirksvorstand*). Then I began to involve women because, from the start, it was apparent that even newly founded political parties were dominated by men. Since then I have been involved in women's issues within the SPD. I was elected to the People's Chamber (*Volkskammer*) in March 1990, and in the East Berlin elections in May I was asked to join the newly formed *Magistrat.*

Our task was considerably different from that of all the other areas in the *Magistrat.* The others had something to administer, structures to change, things to privatize, or, in the area of culture, decisions to make about what should be kept. We didn't have anything to get rid of—no institutions, nothing—so our task was planning and reaching out to the public. We organized a series of seminars or workshops on women and the job market and brought together academics from the field of economics. Then of course we tried to create some new structures for women of the kind that have existed in West Berlin since the early seventies. Our main task was to provide financial support for various projects such as women's shelters or job-retraining seminars. We also organized a seminar on rape with a broad spectrum of participants, including psychotherapists and gynecologists, women from the women's shelters and the police. During the discussion of this very difficult subject it was obvious how great the need is for reflection, which was not possible before.

We provided legal counseling, which addressed what was really the main problem here—this terrible insecurity with regard to one's rights. This was very important because the courts, which themselves were uncertain about their future, sometimes gave out wrong or confusing information, especially in the case of women who were fired from their jobs. It was important that women have a place where they could go to find out if their information was correct. What we were able to do was certainly not very spectacular, but I think it helped. Work has already begun to combine our area within the *Magistrat* with the Department of Family, Women, and Youth in the West Berlin Senate.

Contact between East and West women was established very quickly after the *Wende,* and in many cases the contacts went well. However, there were disagreements, and sometimes the West women dominated the meetings and didn't give the East women an opportunity to talk. But I think that during the process of unification women treated each other very well, better than the men treated them. They talked about their difficulties, and men hardly ever do that. It's very refreshing to have these new discussions between East and West women.

But there are differences. Women in the former GDR haven't learned yet that they have to create a lobby. They still act as individuals and compete against each other instead of doing what men have always done, which is to agree on one person to represent them. I think this will change, but it is important for women to organize so we can elect more women to public office.

Women in the GDR were not emancipated in the sense that is understood in the West. But then the men weren't either. The problem is that in the West people mean something very different when they talk about emancipation than people do in the East. In the West emancipated women are thought of as economically independent, able to make decisions for themselves about their lives. From the point of view of the West, women in the GDR were emancipated because most of them had an independent income. Many women in the West would like to divorce but can't because they are financially dependent on their husbands. Here women were able to divorce and did.

But emancipation means more than that. It means that a woman can determine for herself her place in society, and that didn't happen here. What is astounding is that women's economic independence didn't affect the traditional understanding of gender roles, that women were always responsible for children. That was so ingrained that men weren't allowed to have jobs as day care workers. In the last few years maybe three or four men were allowed into those positions. I'm afraid that at first the conservative understanding of gender roles will continue. There are some who want a change and others who don't. But that's normal. The idea of freedom to choose between work and family is very limited. I can only choose to stay home if I have a husband to finance my choice. Otherwise it's not much fun to stay home and be dependent on welfare programs.

It is a rumor that people were pressured to join the Party. I never was pressured. Of course people in the Party had better opportunities, but people decided for themselves whether to have a particular career and pay the price of membership in the SED, or else to say, no, I won't go along. Everyone was free to make that choice. I think this has been exaggerated; no one was ever killed because she didn't join the SED.

In general I see the events of the past year as positive. That doesn't mean that we won't have very serious social conflicts in the future. Perhaps other people who are more interested in their personal security see things differently than I do, less adventuresome people who aren't as willing to take risks, or who perhaps have fewer skills. I think that many people from the GDR are not well suited for this new society, and they will have a very hard time of it. We have to pay attention that they don't get lost.

I've noticed that anyone who was active during this time sees things somewhat differently than those people who stood by, helpless and abandoned, and felt the stream of history wash over them. This may be one of the reasons I'm optimistic. I've been able to participate in the changes and haven't been forced to watch passively from the sidelines. I'm so glad that it all happened.

July 1992

After the all-German elections on December 2, 1990, the East Berlin Magistrat *ceased to exist, and Eva Kunz lost her job. However, because of her high profile in the area of women's issues she was able to find another position where she could put her experience to good use. She was appointed to the Department of Women in the Ministry of Work, Welfare, Health, and Women in the new Brandenburg state government. She found great satisfaction in her work, but she acknowledged the difficulty of trying to put in place women's policy without the support of an active women's movement. "The pressure from the grass roots isn't there," she said.*

One of the things she missed from the GDR was the time to cultivate relationships and read challenging books. Her time was consumed by her work. Nevertheless, she made clear that she had not fallen into GDR-nostalgia. She smiled, "I couldn't be pessimistic even if I tried. I love life too much."

Because she had not been allowed to travel to the West before the Wende, *her recent trips to Paris and London had left lasting impressions in her mind. Having observed what she called the conscious education of an elite in Cambridge, she smiled, "At least there they did it with a touch of class."*

Katharina Stillisch,

forty-eight, press secretary for Eva Kunz, Office of Equal Opportunity, *Magistrat*

December 1990

My interview with Katharina Stillisch occurred quite by chance. When I arrived at the Office of Equal Opportunity at the Magistrat, *my scheduled appointment with Commissioner Eva Kunz had been cancelled, so her press secretary, Katharina Stillisch, volunteered to give what became a highly spirited interview.*

The first question—whether women were the losers of unification—was greeted with a torrent of words. For an hour Katharina Stillisch spoke in biting and at times sarcastic tones about the situation of GDR *women since the* Wende. *Of the six female journalists at the local newspaper where she had worked before the* Wende, *four had been fired, while most of the men had remained. Although* GDR *law stipulated equality of the sexes, men were "a little more equal" than women. She added that the* GDR *created a false emancipation for women: they were guaranteed many of the same rights as men, but in addition to their work outside the home, they were expected to shoulder the extra burden of family and household. Katharina Stillisch articulated the widespread ambivalence toward the notion of emancipation among* GDR *women. On the one hand, she acknowledged the value of work: women found self-respect and a sense of community through their work. She herself would not have wanted to give it up. On the other hand, the double burden of work and family was too much for women.*

Katharina Stillisch was considered by her colleagues to be strong and outspoken. She was active in SPD *party politics and held local public office. With the dissolution of the* Magistrat *and unemployment only a few days away, she looked forward to devoting more time to her political work.*

44

Katharina Stillisch

On May 6, 1990 I was elected to be an SPD representative to the district parliament from Treptow in East Berlin (*Bezirksverordnete*). I am considered a strong woman. I am capable, and I accomplish a lot. When our SPD party head (*Fraktionsvorsitzender*) resigned from that office, two candidates came forward as possible replacements, a weak man and I. You can imagine who was elected. He only got three more votes than I did, but the weak man was elected. In Treptow we have thirty-eight people representing the SPD and of those, only seven are women. Men don't want women in leading positions—and certainly not capable women—because they are afraid of such women. We are being pushed into a situation again into which we have always been pushed: a woman must be twice as good as a man in order to get anywhere.

For example, of the thirty-one male SPD representatives, none has volunteered for any training workshops, but two of the seven women have. None of the thirty-one men has been in a rhetoric course, but two of the seven women have. This is typical. Just because he's a man he has an advantage. Our men have learned this lesson in the last six months extremely well.

The men all earned more, especially if they were in the Party, and they had more opportunities than women before the *Wende*. Especially in my profession, which is a typical Party profession. Journalism was a profession made up almost exclusively of people in the Party. There were very few people who weren't in a party. Either they were in the SED or in a block party. The block parties such as the CDU went along with the SED, but no one speaks about this. The people from our CDU simply moved over into the West German CDU and no one seems to be interested in what they did before.

Women in GDR politics played exactly the same role that they play now. Token women. In the *Politbüro* there were only two women, Margot Honecker and one other. Inge Lange was head of the German Democratic Women's Association (*Demokratischer Frauenbund Deutschlands*, DFD). It was the men who made policy. On a local level it was the same as on the national level, and today it doesn't look any better. I must also say it doesn't look any better even in my own party, the SPD. Men make policy, and when a woman becomes too strong, the men try to vote her out as soon as possible. In my district four men were put up for the all-Berlin parliamentary elections on December 2 and not a single woman. If Eva Kunz had wanted Internal Affairs instead of Equal Opportunity she wouldn't have become City Commissioner. Look at the *Magistrat*. Of the only two women in the *Magistrat*, one is in Equal Opportunity, the other in the Ministry of Culture. I don't have to tell you how badly culture is viewed. Culture is always the fifth wheel on the cart.

The Department of Equal Opportunity is concerned with Article 3 of the constitution, which states that women and men are equal. However, we exist because, of course, women and men are *not* equal. There are still some who are a little more equal, and those are the men. We lived in a false emancipation, a *Scheinemanzipation*. Women had equal rights, but they didn't have equal rights. In order to look after and protect women's interests, new positions to represent women's issues (*Frauenbeauftragte*) were introduced through the Round Table, and at the same time the Department for Equal Opportunity was created in the *Magistrat*.

We support work on various projects, for example two houses for battered women. One is supported by the Protestant church, the *Frauenhaus Bora*, and the other is an autonomous house. These never existed in the GDR. It was taboo to talk about violence against women. It certainly existed, but significantly less than it does now since the *Wende*. I can't judge violence in marriage, but there was certainly as much as in the West. And it's for these women that the houses are being built. But there has been a tremendous increase in violence against women on the street—violence such as rape.

Women's projects have sprung up everywhere since the *Wende*. There were no real women's projects before the *Wende*. We had the German Democratic Women's Association, which slid into becoming a knitting and crocheting circle at the end. Forty years ago it was conceptualized differently, for the emancipation of women. What we had was a false emancipation, never a real one. Women weren't respected, as the elections showed.

But women did have rights. They had equal rights in the area of work where they could pursue any career they wanted. Girls were encouraged to go into areas such as mechanics and engineering. We always needed workers, and there was no question that women should work. Before the *Wende* we had a large number of women working. Women also had a right to a space for their children in day care, supported by the state. That made things much easier for working women. We also had a large number of single mothers because women were told they could be mothers even if they weren't married. And it functioned well.

I've found that all of a sudden a lot of younger women now want to stay home because it is too difficult to have a small child, to work, and to deal with all the other details. It's too much. From my experience, it was very, very difficult to manage everything. The younger women haven't noticed what is in store for them. They don't get it. When children are small, of course it's nice to be able to stay home. When my son was very little I didn't want to take him to *Kinderkrippe,* but I had to work. These young women don't know how difficult it is going to be to get a job later because men are moving into these jobs. Before, women could stop working for a short period of time if, for example, their child was little and their husbands earned a fairly good income, and then they could go back to work with no problem. There were always jobs to be found and mothers had to be hired. Firms couldn't say, "You have a small child who will be sick a lot and therefore we don't want you." The firms had to hire them. And now the firms are saying no.

I'm a case in point. I wanted to stay home with my babies, but my son went to *Kinderkrippe* when he was two months old. That was before the new policy which allowed new mothers to stay home for a whole year. Back then it was only two months. At that point I would have liked to work only half-time in order to take care of my son's health. Otherwise I liked going to work, but I'm not a typical mother. Most mothers want to stay home with their babies. I would have liked to be home when he started school too, maybe working half-days, but otherwise I like to work far too much to have stayed home the whole time. Work is very important to me. The only reason I can contemplate being unemployed now is because I have so much to do as a district representative that it's like a job for me. I couldn't imagine a life without work.

Women in the GDR never were aware of the meaning of their work. People simply worked. We grew up, we worked and there wasn't anything else. Since the services for children existed and women couldn't be fired, it was all very convenient. Now women here will have to become much more conscious of work, and I think women will become increasingly dissatisfied. The first thing they will miss is the joy of working. Women will notice how much they miss working when work is no longer available.

The second thing that women haven't realized yet is the economic independence that we enjoyed. When I see something I like I can buy it; it's my money. If I have to eat inexpensively for a whole week because I bought an expensive dress, that's my business. I want to be independent. That has nothing to do with love and marriage. Economic dependence is more likely to ruin such things.

It all goes back to the fact that housework is not valued. It's not valued by many men. If it were, men would say, "You're working at home and you are entitled to so much of my salary." Then a woman wouldn't have to ask. But this doesn't exist anywhere. In any case housework wouldn't satisfy me. I wouldn't look down on my husband if he stayed home and I went to work. Everyone should work according to his or her capabilities and do what he or she wants. And if a man wants to stay at home, why not? But that is a situation we might achieve in one or two hundred years. It's almost inconceivable now that a man should stay at home. But women think it's normal for them to stay at home, maybe out of habit.

The women's projects that are springing up all over have become a bit fashionable. I think they're necessary, don't misunderstand me. But in the former GDR we didn't need these projects as much as they were needed, for example, in the FRG, because so much social tension was taken care of at work; women were able to come together there and talk about their problems. I miss my colleagues who I worked with for sixteen years, not because I absolutely had to have their friendship, but because we knew each other. My colleagues participated in my divorce, and I helped another colleague with her divorce. We helped each other. What women in the West called self-help groups we had at work. It was taken for granted, and it was one of the reasons women liked to work so much. A lot of this sense of community will be lost.

The *Magistrat* also created a center for counseling women on how to enter the Berlin job market. This office is also responsible for lesbian and gay issues, although we didn't do much with that. This is all very new and hasn't been talked about much yet. Time was too short: from May to December, only seven months. The *Magistrat* was supposed to start a lesbian and gay house, which I personally didn't think was such a great idea since it would mean a further marginalization. We have to reach a point in our society where all lifestyles are taken for granted and are integrated into society.

I am "red" and I am on the left, but the SED wasn't for me. I always thought like a Social Democrat and as soon as the SPD was founded in the East—it was called SDP at first—there was no question but that I would join. In addition, I always wanted to change things. I saw a lot that needed to be done in the district, and I wanted to help get it done. For sure, I won't give up, even if our men in the district don't love me very much right now. I also work with the Committee for Equal Opportunity, of course, to try to do something for women, and we've gotten some lumps and bumps, but we won't give up.

July 1992

When the East Berlin Magistrat was dissolved after the all-Berlin elections on December 2, 1990, Katharina Stillisch lost her job. For six months she received unemployment benefits—68 percent of her previous salary—and came to the realization that people developed greater self-respect when a government subsidized their employment (as had been the case in the GDR) than when it subsidized their unemployment (as in capitalist Germany).

Taking advantage of her political network, she joined a group of SPD women in forming an organization to help women find their way into the job market. The group was granted ABM money for one year and opened a job information center as well as a training center, where women were taught skills necessary to land a job. Katharina Stillisch was its director. A stack of books on the table was testimony to the new reading she had done to prepare herself for teaching these classes. She said she had never worked so hard in her life—up to twelve hours a day—but she knew she offered a program of high quality: "I have the knowledge of the Wessis but speak the language of the Ossis."

Because the work load in her new job was so overwhelming, she had given up her position as local representative in Treptow. She was sorry to leave public office because she thought that women's voices were being lost in the return to patriarchal politics as usual. However, she believed one had to work from within the power structure in order to change it and hoped to seek public office again sometime in the future.

Katharina Stillisch thought many GDR citizens had come through the Wende with expectations that were too high. The postwar years, which she could still remember, had been far worse than this period of uncertainty. She looked forward to the opportunity to make a success of her new job but at the same time wondered whether, at fifty-one, she could manage it.

Karin Tittmann,

thirty-nine, physical therapist at the Charité Hospital

March 1991

When Karin Tittmann and her husband went to meetings of New Forum during the autumn of 1989, they left their apartment separately so that if one of them were arrested the other could still care for the children. Karin Tittmann had never been in the political opposition before—she was too busy raising a family—but she became caught up in the energy of the fledgling democracy movement, asserting that nothing in the world could have held her back.

As a mother, she was particularly interested in working for educational reform. As part of a parents' group within New Forum, she met with teachers to demand that, among other things, the military tanks be removed from the toy collection at day care. The parents also agitated for greater flexibility in the rigid school curriculum. Liberalizing the educational system was important because it was the schools, after all, that taught future citizens of the GDR to conform to the image that the state prescribed for them.

When she herself was in school, Karin Tittmann's classmates called her "the saint" because she went to church. Children in the GDR, she claimed, learned that the proper attitude toward traditional religion was derision; they were taught that a real socialist was an atheist. However, she continued her church activities into adulthood—despite disadvantages to herself and her family.

Talking with her in her work environment at the Charité Hospital, I was taken by her personal warmth and youthful energy. She was striking in her exuberant optimism about the Wende.

Karin Tittmann

The *Wende* started for me when I got involved in politics. I had never done anything like that before because I was busy raising my children. Besides I didn't think I would be able to change anything, and I couldn't identify with any of the parties. Then I learned from relatives that there was this new group. It didn't have a name yet, but it was the beginnings of New Forum. I decided to go and hear what they had to say. That was in August 1989.

The meetings were watched pretty carefully. When my husband and I left the house in the evening, we went separately so that if one of us got arrested the other wouldn't be. That's the kind of thing we thought about at the beginning. Someone was always present at the meetings with a tape recorder or to write down every word that was said. They knew everything that was going on. When we came outside at midnight there were always two or three people standing there taking down our names. It was all very official—they didn't try to hide. The people at the Berlin meetings turned out to be the nucleus of New Forum— Bärbel Bohley, Jens Reich, Ingrid Köppe, and people like that. At first we met in people's apartments, but the movement grew so fast that apartments weren't big enough.

Every day there was a demonstration or a meeting at the church. We wanted to organize a force that could make change from the bottom up, without fear. We met on Tuesdays—eighty people in a two-room apartment, two meetings in every district in Berlin. I had the feeling that the entire population was being mobilized. Nothing in the world could have held us back. We all wanted the same thing: not to be locked up here anymore, to be free, to be treated more justly, and to decide things for ourselves. People are now so overwhelmed with the new bureaucracy that they have no time or energy for anything else.

In Neuenhagen where I live we had meetings at my home, and we told people what had been said at the meetings in Berlin. But the meetings got too large for our apartment so we started meeting in a room at the church. That was November 1989. I avoided the sit-down strikes where the police got involved. I was too scared. I heard that the children of parents who were getting arrested were put in orphanages, and that was terrifying to me. It might have been extremely difficult to get out of jail if I had been arrested because of the arbitrariness with which people were held and released.

November 9 was actually funny. We were visiting some friends. People were constantly talking openly with each other at markets and on the streets—

making new friends had never been so easy. It was all very new. So we were at friends, watching the news on TV to see whether there had been any new violence. We got home about 11:00 P.M. and turned on the TV again and heard that the border was open. I said, "Do we have any gas in the car? Let's go! I have to see it!" So we got into the car, picked up some students along the way and at 1:30 A.M. we were at the border. There were four lanes of cars waiting to get through. It took us an hour. They stamped our I.D., but instead of stamping it in the back, they put the stamp across my picture. Everyone looked at their identification cards and saw that the same thing had been done to all of them. I said, "Oh no, they'll never let us back in." Our kids didn't know where we were—they were asleep when we left—and I had to be at work the next morning at 7:00.

We got through the border. Everyone was beating on the roof of the car. There were thousands of people everywhere, yelling, passing around champagne. We wanted to go to the Ku'Damm, West Berlin's busy shopping street, and as we unrolled the window to ask a taxi driver how to get there, someone shoved a newspaper in with a colored picture of the open border. We couldn't believe it. I still have the newspaper at home. We drove to Cafe Kranzler, parked the car somewhere, got out, and there was a reporter from *Newsweek* who asked me in English what I was feeling, and I said something, and he asked if he could print it, and I said yes. We all decided to meet back at 3:30 in order to get back by 6:00. People were dancing; we couldn't move—it was like Carnival in Rio. Two older people came up to me and took me by the arm. I asked them why they weren't in bed at this hour. They said this day would only come once in a century, and they couldn't possibly sleep. Then we met three guys, American, Dutch, and French. They asked us lots of questions and invited us to a party a week later.

It was strange for me being in West Berlin. As I was standing in front of Cafe Kranzler, I remembered back to August 11, 1961, two days before the Wall went up. I was ten years old. We had just come home from a camping trip. My parents knew something was going to happen and talked about staying in the West. I didn't understand what they were talking about. They said, "We have everything we need, the whole family is together." But they went back because of my grandparents. I remember seeing a black person for the first time. I went up to him and licked his arm to see if he tasted like chocolate. My parents were so embarrassed they apologized profusely, and he reached into his pocket and gave me a handful of candy. Those were my memories of West Berlin, and here I was standing there again after all that time.

After the Wall opened, New Forum continued to meet and talk about how to structure the new society. One of the New Forum groups talked about hospitals and homes for the elderly; others discussed how schools could be changed. The strict curriculum at school didn't allow for any individual choice. There was no possibility of changing the curriculum for weak students—no support for them. It was too uniform for me. I was active in the parents' group, which met with the teachers on a regular basis. We tried to get the teachers to deviate from the strict course of study. We also wanted them to leave out some subjects. In civics class the kids had to study elections in the GDR. If the kids told the truth and said, "There are no real elections in the GDR," they flunked. Some teachers simply didn't bring up the topic and chose another nonpolitical topic instead, but that took courage. The same thing with history. Eighth-grade history was simply not accurate.

When my first child was in nursery school I tried to organize the parents to get rid of the tanks the kids were playing with. We discussed it over and over at the school, and finally we just went into the classroom, opened the closet, and took the tanks out. We said, "If you want to keep the tanks we'll take our children home," and they relented. The songs the kids had to sing were all political socialist songs, no songs about springtime or nature. Everything was highly militarized.

I sat for a short while at the Round Table in Neuenhagen as a representative of New Forum; we tried to see what we could change. The SPD and CDU and the Liberals and PDS were all there. We wanted ideas and actions to move from the bottom to the top, and that sounded to outsiders as though we didn't have any ideas at all; we were seen as chaotic. We talked about everything. Things were never again so democratic.

Then in January 1990 there was a division within New Forum into two groups: those people who wanted to have a political party, and those who didn't. There was a big public meeting with TV cameras. That was when I got out. I was willing to work for schools or hospitals or whatever people wanted me to work for, but not within a party. I continued to sympathize with their goals and I voted for them. If we had had more time and if the CDU hadn't come along with all their money and promised the world, things might have been different.

Of course I was happy that the Wall fell, and I still am today. I'm a very optimistic person, but I also still have my job. I've seen the problems in families where both people are out of work, the psychological burden that we never knew before, this uncertainty. But my job isn't completely secure either. I'm one of the few here who work only six hours instead of eight. If they start firing people I'll be among the first to go. My husband will probably be unemployed come summer. He has a degree in engineering and works in a firm that was taken over by a West German company, Siemens. He's supposed to sell computers, but he hasn't sold a single one since September. If he loses his job I'll be working, and he'll take care of the children.

My father was self-employed, so I wasn't allowed to get my high school diploma, even though I had good grades. Only the children of workers or the intelligentsia could finish high school. So I finished a technical training program and then got my diploma a year later. It wasn't my fault that my father wasn't a blue-collar worker.

I started going to church as a child. My family was involved in the church, and I never saw any reason to leave. My parents were never in a party—they weren't involved in politics. The church was always open to young people and opposition groups. Of course I had problems at school. My brother did too. On Wednesdays there were always the meetings of the Young Pioneers, the Party's youth organization, and I was the only one who went to Christian lessons. I actually went to both, which wasn't very consistent. The kids at school called me "the saint." It bothered me a little bit, just like it bothered me when I had to start wearing glasses in the first grade and when my mother gave me a strange haircut, but it never bothered me for long. I wasn't a complicated child.

My friends were always people from church. I had very few relationships with people in the Party. At first I tried to ignore the entire subject of political affiliation and just accept people for who they were with their strong points and weak points. My first husband was in the Party. We decided not to make an issue out of it, but when we started having kids, things got complicated. At first he said, "Send them all to church and I won't say anything about the Party." But even though he didn't talk about it, his attitude and his behavior were shaped by his membership in the Party, and our notions about raising the children were so different that after ten years we finally got a divorce. My present husband was in a party, but not in the SED. He was in the Liberal Party, the LDPD, which saw itself almost in opposition to the SED, although people are now saying they were the same as the SED. We got married in church, but we weren't able to have our children baptized then. They are all baptized now, and this Sunday they will be confirmed.

I think people who were active in the church were perhaps more courageous than many. Those of us in the church always felt that we formed a kind of opposition to the state. Starting when I was a child, I felt safe in church and at the same time part of the opposition. The closer we got to the *Wende* and the more opportunity we saw to make change, the stronger our opposition became. This opposition manifested itself in open discussions about topics such as homosexuality, AIDS, and sex education—all of which were taboo in public. The church sponsored evenings where reports were given about things that were intentionally kept secret by the state. The pastors were usually young men, and the congregations were small. In Neuenhagen, a district of thirteen thousand inhabitants, there were ten of us who regularly went to church and were involved in church activities. At our church the lesson from the Bible was read every week, but instead of basing the sermon on that passage, the pastor would take a particular political subject and apply the Bible to it.

Before the *Wende*, we had lots of readings at church from forbidden books. I remember specifically the time when Wolf Biermann was exiled in 1976. Lots of writers and other artists came together in an act of solidarity and declared that they couldn't continue to live and work under these conditions. There was very little room for creativity. It was very hard to get your hands on books that went against the grain. Maybe if you had a friend who worked in a book store you could get books by people like Christa Wolf. It was all under the table. Sometimes retired people went over to West Berlin and brought us back some. We took the books to church where we discussed them and passed them back and forth. We couldn't get things by GDR writers let alone from the United States. If we did get American literature, it was always in English, which meant that most people couldn't read it. We could read Goethe and Schiller and the socialist writers, but we couldn't get Hermann Hesse.

One time our pastor invited Stefan Heym to come and speak, and Heym read from a book that was forbidden. The Stasi were there taking notes. Usually the Stasi weren't very interested in what was going on. They were just there, and everyone knew which ones they were because they didn't fit in. But this time the pastor openly welcomed them. He said, "I welcome among our guests the spies from the state security. I think it will be an interesting evening; please write down every word." Two days later he was invited to Stasi headquarters and given two choices: either he could go to jail for nine years or he could apply

to leave the country. He decided to try to leave. That was November 1986.
On Christmas Eve, he suddenly received his permission to go and was given
twenty-four hours to get out of the country. He had lots of books and things
and hadn't even begun to pack. The entire congregation went over to his house
with boxes and baskets and bags, and his whole household was packed up in
twenty-four hours. He went to West Berlin and for two years he wasn't able to
have a congregation. Now he's back in Neuenhagen with his family. The kids
never wanted to go to West Berlin.

Some people had to leave the church if their job required that they join the
Party. If they wanted to become the director of a plant or a factory they were
required to be in the Party, and the Party and the church didn't go together. A
real socialist was an atheist. I think the idea of socialism is terrific, and if it could
ever be realized, it would be completely compatible with a belief in God. But
socialism has never been realized the way Marx and Engels conceived it.

July 1992

*Karin Tittmann's life seemed at first glance little changed since March 1991. Still
holding her job at the Charité, she was as optimistic as before. However, West
German heirs of a former owner of her house had made application to reclaim it.
They had never seen the house, nor did they want to live in it; they desired only
monetary compensation.*

*Her husband had lost his job, and although he received a stipend for the
retraining program he had enrolled in, she was now the primary breadwinner.
"We've reversed roles," she said. "He doesn't like it so much, but the new situation
is actually harder for me." Her thirty-hour-a-week job at the Charité had increased to full time and—with the new financial responsibility for the family
welfare—no longer felt to her like a hobby. The additional hours meant less time
with her children who needed more direction now, "more time to discuss the
changes caused by the Wende."*

*Karin Tittmann still saw the Wende as positive. The opportunity to visit friends
and relatives in Austria, Switzerland, and Canada had only increased her enthusiasm because "life had gained a third dimension, the spatial one." Furthermore the
Wende had brought her what she had always wanted: the chance to use therapy
methods that were unknown in the GDR, such as Shiatsu and Chi Gong. She
complained that even yoga and karate had been discouraged because the state*

"was afraid of what would happen if so many people came together and thought."
In addition, private practice had become a new option.

   She believed that the desire for freedom had sparked the demonstrations in the
fall of 1989 and was sorry that money seemed to have become the new focus. Seeing
that young people who were not raised to be materialistic were becoming so, she
hoped that her children would hold onto the values she had taught them.

Eva Stahl,

forty-three, administrator in the
City Agency for Foreigners
(*Ausländerbeauftragte*)

February 1991

Eva Stahl was a fighter. A mother of two children, she fought the educational system in the GDR which she said was "an instrument of oppression that crippled the children morally and intellectually." She maintained that the children in GDR schools developed character traits she viewed as negative, such as the "desire to be part of the group, fear of being an individual." In addition, Eva Stahl fought the parents of her children's classmates who refused to discuss or consider "the topic of fascism in the GDR" or to admit that they were participants in a corrupt system that was harmful to their children. She resisted her own parents who would not allow her, unmarried and pregnant, to come home unless she lied to friends and family that the father of her child had been killed in a plane crash.

Eva Stahl was forced to fight because, as she put it, she was "a strong, independent woman," and women like her were often seen as a threat to those who wanted to maintain the status quo. In addition, she was a single mother. Contrary to the officially propagated view that women with children, whether married or single, had equal chances in GDR society, she said that single mothers like herself were subjected to considerable discrimination. In general, women were able to achieve roughly as much as men, she said, "which wasn't very much," but single mothers were less respected than their married counterparts. She noticed this lack of recognition when she talked with the teachers at school: "If both parents or just the father came to talk to the teacher, it had a different effect than if a single mother came." She maintained that, despite the state's attempt to glorify motherhood, "the hard work of raising children was not valued in this society."

Now Eva Stahl looks forward to a future where professional expectations will be higher and, in contrast to the way things were in the GDR, people will have to think

about what they want. The Wende *took away her "fear of thinking about things."*
For her it was a liberation.

Eva Stahl

I suffered most of all in this society because the educational system was so bad. Intolerable living conditions made us move a lot, so the kids went to various schools. At one school a parents' committee had to be elected, and I was the only one who spoke up and voiced my opinion about anything. No one supported me. In fact, I was labeled "abnormal" in front of the entire teachers' collective.

I remember a similar situation two years ago at work where I brought up the topic of fascism in the GDR. I can still see my colleagues physically going after me. Particularly the women didn't understand what I was talking about. I asked them, where were you all the years when your kids were going to day care and nursery school? Didn't you see the psychological brutality that your kids were subjected to? I can't understand how these women could think the system was good. One woman came after me with her purse, and two people held her back, but no one supported me, no one talked to me. It was hard, and I must say I particularly blame the women. I wonder where the people were back then who are now talking about how badly treated they were. Where were they then? I have a hard time with the people who are claiming to be victims of the system because I never met any of them. I know these people as parents and as colleagues, and no one was there when I expressed any sort of critical opinion. Even though they had the opportunity, they kept quiet so they wouldn't hurt their children's future or the chances of a raise at work. There was a great silence. Even worse, these so-called victims actually played up to the teachers.

Many unpleasant things happened in the last several years. For one, my son had psoriasis on his head, and the doctor recommended that he get his hair cut very short. We had just moved into a new area, so my son started school there with his short hair, and the kids gave him trouble. He also refused to wear his FDJ shirt during roll call. For one thing, he didn't want to wear the FDJ shirt because it didn't breathe. As a single mother with two children, I could only afford the cheapest kind. Besides that, I had persuaded him not to submit to the requirement. I always tried to get the kids to think for themselves. But I also told them that even if they were right, they had to develop the art of getting along because we would always be weaker in a confrontation with the state.

The school officials, all women, noticed that my son wasn't wearing his FDJ shirt to roll call and wasn't attending parts of the FDJ program. It wasn't actually because he wanted to miss the FDJ program. He was attending a music school and had performances during the times of some of the FDJ political instruction. As a result some of the teachers—also women—singled him out. People looked at me and said that I should see to it that my kids got to the FDJ events. My son's teacher accused him of being a political opponent: he wore his hair short, he refused to wear his FDJ shirt. He bordered on "Americanized behavior." That's the way the teacher described it. My son was in the eighth grade. I let it go, but I kept my eye on the teacher. He wrote a report in which he said that my son opposed the socialist system, which influenced his chances for a job later. The report wasn't accurate. My son had worked outside of school—he helped remove garbage and worked in the gardens around the apartment complex—but he didn't tell the teacher because it seemed beneath his dignity somehow. I think he was a good boy, a good citizen, but at school kids were judged only according to their official, registered activities. So I went to the music school and asked them to write a letter in support of my son. They did that, but the teacher got worse. My son put his briefcase in the wrong place in the classroom, and the teacher threw it down the stairs.

The situation at Mark's school got so bad that I went to the school authorities and on bended knee begged that my daughter be allowed to change schools so she wouldn't fall into the hands of this teacher. It became an event in that small town because it wasn't common to change schools; you had to have good reasons. All the teachers in the area closed ranks, and my daughter was singled out at her new school. My daughter sometimes made inappropriate political statements. For example, when she was asked at school what was the highest representative of the people, she answered "the *Bundestag*" (the West German Parliament). That got around and the kids and I all felt the discrimination. This is just one more example of the thousands of problems we had over the years.

When the male students got a little older they were brought together to talk about their future service in the military. A representative of the army came to school to talk to the boys. My son had stated that he would be willing to serve for three years because if he did, he could be assured a place at the university. We knew he would be asked why he didn't want to serve for ten years. He would be told that the material advantages were great, and he could finish his university degree at the same time he was serving in the army. So we had prepared an answer, which he gave in the presence of the director of the school, who was also a woman. He said his mother was a single parent and after many years of raising her children alone, she wanted to have him at home.

He came home and refused to talk to me for days. The army man had said in front of the entire group of boys something to the effect that they were all old enough to decide for themselves whether they wanted to join up for ten years or not, but Mark was still tied to his mother's apron strings. These were boys fourteen or fifteen years old. As a result my son said he wasn't going to join up for even three years. He was going to do only the required time. He went into his room and closed the door and wouldn't talk to me.

I realized only too late that the children were systematically educated at school to go against their parents: my teacher said this and this, and what you say is wrong. The teachers played the kids off against their parents, particularly when the parents were critical and most especially when the parent was a critical, fairly independent woman. I think the schools were an instrument of oppression. They crippled the children morally and intellectually. The kids developed certain character traits: fear of peer opinion, desire to be part of the group, fear of being an individual. The teachers and parents who worked together were often not even SED members. The power structures that existed were harmful to everybody, but it's the children I feel sorry for.

There are issues I have to work on personally, especially since I was a member of our Party right up until the end of 1990. I wanted to get out much earlier, but I didn't know what kind of repercussions there would be for my children. In 1988 I did have the courage to drop my subscription to the newspaper *Neues Deutschland*, "the voice of the Party." I actually would have been willing to submit to the harassment that would have come if I had dropped out of the Party, even jail, but I didn't know what would happen to the children.

I suffered tremendously as a result of what my children were subjected to, and I still suffer. It hurt me. I learned during all the years of socialism that a mother must take responsibility for her children; no one can do that for her. On the other hand, the facilities that looked so good, such as day care and nursery school, caused me to doubt my own abilities as a mother and to place my trust in the officially supported facilities. We were told how important it was for our children to go to day care, how important it was for them to play with other children. I never heard anyone say that these facilities were anything but good. I think it's simply wrong for women to give their children to complete strangers to raise. I think women can help their kids to be able to develop real human relationships and in this way they contribute to world peace.

I'm so happy that kids are now going to be able to choose which school they want to go to and don't have simply to do what they are told. The individual desires of students will receive more attention now. If Mark doesn't want to take Russian, which is hard for him, he doesn't have to anymore. My kids got good grades, but they turned off, tuned out. They didn't really learn anything. There was a big discrepancy between their grades and their real accomplishments.

When I was twenty-one I had my first child. I was at college and I couldn't find a place for us to live. I had to waitress on weekends in order to stretch my stipend. It was then that I experienced how single women were discriminated against when they had a child. A woman in this socialist system could achieve as much as a man, which wasn't very much, and so I wouldn't say that women in general experienced discrimination. I think they were treated fairly equally. But women with children had a different experience. It made a difference that I wasn't married. I had the feeling that I wasn't respected or recognized, for example, at school with Mark's teacher. If both parents or just the father came to talk to the teacher, it had a different effect than if a single mother came. It is ironic that, as women, these teachers had no respect for a single mother. The schools also subtly supported the traditional belief that housework belonged to the mother. I was appalled to find statements in my children's reading material such as, "I help my mother with the dishes."

I also got used to being called a whore. When I was pregnant, my parents wouldn't let me come home. It was Christmas. My grandfather raised me, not my parents, and at the moment when I really needed them they forbade me access to the house. No one was supposed to know that I was pregnant. So I had to stay at school. I kept trying to contact my parents, but I was allowed to visit only if I agreed to say that the father of my children was an honorable man who had been killed in an airplane accident. My parents were prejudiced their entire lives.

For some reason, I wasn't affected by their prejudices. I began studying foreign languages in school and was always interested in foreigners. Nearby there was an institute for tropical agriculture, and a number of black Africans who spoke fluent English and French were studying there. My language teacher would invite them to gatherings at school, and usually another girl and I were the only Germans present. We would sometimes walk through town—it was a small town outside Berlin—and people talked about us. I didn't let it bother me and would intentionally appear in public with the Africans. But people said I was a bad woman. I never had an intimate relationship with the Africans. Later when I was working in Berlin, I was considered suspect because of my contact with foreigners. Once I went to the theater with someone from Belgium, and I had to be sure to report it because if I didn't someone might see me and report me. These contacts with foreigners were collected in a file on me, my so-called *Kaderakte*, which followed me everywhere. With time it all got to be too much, and I eventually gave up all contact with foreigners. I don't think the discrimination against foreigners has changed since the *Wende*. It's just that now it can be openly expressed. There was a lack of respect for a different culture, a lack of knowledge. The GDR exported bicycles to other countries and never had enough for our children, and people blamed the foreigners. They blamed them when things were scarce because they were weaker and unprotected. What's happening right now with the extreme hatred against foreigners is just what happened within our socialist system: an absolute intolerance of anyone who thinks or acts differently from the norm. I experienced this intolerance myself, and as a result I withdrew. I thought for a long time that I couldn't live here because I suffered so much. But I didn't take the next step. I would have liked to apply for an exit visa, but I would never have gotten my children out. Plus I always hoped that the political system would improve.

In my divorce proceedings I almost lost my daughter to my husband. The judge was a woman and was so delighted that a man wanted custody of his children that she almost ruled against me, despite a number of significant factors. A man who was interested in his children was valued more highly than a woman was because such a situation was so rare. Women weren't recognized; they were considered inferior. They had to take care of their children and their household, and they had to hold down a job because they had to earn money. The harder you worked, the less time you had for your kids. It was a vicious circle. Men usually avoided their responsibilities as fathers because they wanted to devote more time to getting ahead at work. When I think about those years I feel very tired. The hard work of raising children was not valued in this society.

Before the *Wende* I worked as a French translator for the news service, and often worked the night shift—which created an interesting variant on how to come to terms with my being a single parent with two children. I could go shopping early in the morning and buy things such as pumpernickel bread which was gone from the shelves when workers came home in the evening. I liked the job because I could read about things in the international press that weren't printed here. For example, AIDS. We didn't have AIDS here, supposedly. Reading the international press gave me an entirely different perspective from the one available to socialist correspondents. I got to the point where I didn't know what to believe and ended up not believing anything. That's when my critical attitude really started.

I am very happy that professional expectations are going to be higher now. I think that when more is expected of people they rise to those expectations. They have to think about where they are going and what they want. Before the *Wende* this sort of thinking wasn't necessary. I'm happy about the new developments because they make higher demands on people. The *Wende* has taken away my fear of thinking about things. It's made me more active, more open for new things, freer. I can only see the *Wende* as a liberation.

July 1992

Several months ago Eva Stahl entered a training program to become a paralegal. She felt fortunate to have found an internship with two attorneys who were concerned with social issues, especially those affecting foreigners. Until December 1991 she still had her job in the City Agency for Foreigners, but she voluntarily walked away from it because of growing dissatisfaction with the new policies and the increasing bureaucratic mentality. She welcomed unemployment as an opportunity for a much needed time for reflection. "Before, I had no choice. I had to work."

She wanted to use this time to come to terms with her past and to ask herself about her own involvement in the system. She was enjoying her new isolation, reading and watching political programs on television. She also planned to process her new insights through writing. One of her most penetrating realizations was just how systematically violence was used by the state. She supported efforts to expose those who had worked for the Stasi, officially and unofficially: "It will create fear in those who should be afraid." No stranger to the pervasive interference of the Stasi in family life, she was denounced by both her husband and her parents who falsely accused her of "having relations" with foreigners. She was forced to break off all private foreign contacts.

Having often turned to wine as an escape, Eva Stahl noticed that after the Wende *she had stopped drinking. Although she didn't understand what had happened, she was pleased to be able to say, "Now I can truly be myself. That wasn't possible before."*

Gerda Maron,

forty-eight, film editor for East German Television (DFF)

February 1991

Gerda Maron's interview illuminates the double bind in which many convinced socialists in the GDR found themselves after the Wende. Because she grew up the daughter of a private craftsman, she was labeled a "capitalist brat" and was discriminated against at school. As a result, she withheld allegiance to the socialist state and never joined the Party. Yet she adhered to socialist ideals which she discovered in her Christian upbringing—tolerance, kindness, and concern for others—and which she missed in the socialism that was practiced in the GDR. She felt that her Christianity made her "more socialist than the socialists." This attitude, plus her decision to study English rather than the politically more acceptable Russian, made her unpopular. However, when the country was turning toward a market economy, she was labeled again, "in the other direction" this time. While some former SED members glibly exchanged socialism for capitalism, Gerda Maron continued to support a socialist ideal, and as a result was called "red." "Now any shade of red is considered Stalinist," she said. In addition, people in the West considered anyone suspect who had worked for state-run television. Her notion of socialism was interpreted as "reactionary" in the GDR and "communist" after the Wende.

As a woman in the GDR, Gerda Maron experienced a further double bind. Although the SED proclaimed equal opportunity for all, and although Gerda Maron praised the state for its attempts in this direction, she nevertheless knew that working women with children were at a professional disadvantage. She realized, as did many other women, that even with state-supported facilities for children, she could not combine raising a child with certain careers. For this reason she exchanged her unpredictable position as a freelance interpreter for an eight-to-five job at the television station. For the same reason she never wanted to assume a position of authority at the station.

Despite the fact that she had never endorsed the SED system, Gerda Maron nonetheless worked for and within the state apparatus, a contradiction which people in the West have difficulty comprehending. However, she was not alone. Many people made the choice not to oppose the state outright but rather to show resistance in subtle ways. For Gerda Maron that meant sneaking politically unacceptable movie scenes past the censors. In her interview she provides an example of the kind of compromise many felt they needed to make in order to live in the authoritarian state.

Gerda Maron was one of many GDR citizens who used English in their work even though they were never allowed to improve their language skills in an English-speaking country. Her English, which she insisted on using during the interview, was remarkably good.

Gerda Maron

I was born in Chemnitz. The name was changed to Karl-Marx-Stadt during the time of the GDR. Now it's called Chemnitz again. That's a sign of the change. The very old generation never called it Karl-Marx-Stadt. To me it was just a name. I think that even after the *Wende* one can still honor Marx because what happened wasn't his fault. We have many more important things to do than just change names. I think it's silly, but the Saxons are very concerned about it. My daughter and I were in Marienbad last summer, in Czechoslovakia, and we met some very nice people from Chemnitz. I wasn't used to calling it Chemnitz yet and kept saying Karl-Marx-Stadt, and finally I had to apologize because I didn't want to hurt their feelings. They reminded me over and over that it was called Chemnitz now. These were people of my generation, maybe younger. I think the reason it was important to them was that they were so strongly opposed to the former regime. They wanted to confirm the *Wende*.

My father was a private craftsman, which was not easy in the 1950s, because he was a capitalist, and I was branded a capitalist brat. He was a very honest man, a very hard-working man, and under very difficult conditions he managed to survive. My parents were strong believers in Christianity before World War II, and they raised me as a Christian, but they came to doubt Christianity during the war when they heard what the Nazis did to the Jews. My very dear mother said, if God allowed that to happen, he is a criminal. But they brought me up as a Christian, which I'm very grateful for. Our present generation was brought up without any beliefs at all, and they're lacking in some human qualities, for example, tolerance, kindness, concern for your neighbor, the things that Christianity teaches you. I think I learned those things, although I don't think I believed very strongly as a child.

In the fifties the state tried to eradicate the church, and many left the church because it wasn't advisable to be a member any more. People like me, who were not very strong believers, were glad to leave. I was happy to be able to sleep in on Sundays. The few who remained in the church were true Christians who were willing to suffer hardships and disadvantages because their faith was so strong. Gradually those few became a political power, and the church did very good things to bring about change in this country. I think that the true believers in Marxism will keep up the faith, just as the Christians did in those forty years.

As a teenager and during my student years I strongly opposed any sort of socialism because of the way the system treated me. I was studying to become a teacher, and although I didn't want to become a teacher I didn't have any choice because I wasn't the child of a worker or a farmer. But I worked hard at the university. I concentrated very hard on German literature and particularly on English, and when I graduated I was offered a position on the faculty. But that was at the University of Jena, and there was a certain Klaus Maron in Berlin with whom I had been in love for many years, and he couldn't come to Jena. So I had to give up my university career and become a high school teacher in Berlin. I liked teaching, but I didn't like the additional political work, the Young Pioneers, the military training, all the things I had to do. So I started studying at Humboldt University and got my degree in English.

Then I did something that one just did not do in the GDR. I quit. This was very serious. If an employer wasn't satisfied with a worker, he had to keep him anyway. If he wanted to get rid of him, he didn't fire him because the worker would never get another job, so he told him to quit. But that meant that he had performed badly. I quit because it was the only way for me to get out of the educational system. They needed teachers so badly that they wouldn't ever allow them to go into another profession. Quitting meant that I wouldn't be able to get another job, so that's why I started working as a freelance interpreter.

Before 1961 my family had the opportunity to leave the GDR, as thousands did, but we decided to stay and improve it. We realized, however, that we could not live in this country and continue to oppose it. It's not possible to do that. We tried to be honest, to get rid of the things we didn't like. I had a critical view of the Party's politics, but I identified with my country. I could never become a Party member because I could never subject myself to the absolute Party discipline, and I didn't want to go to the Party meetings every Monday. When I asked people I knew what they did for two hours at those meetings, they said they just talked rubbish. I thought it was a waste of time. But I tried to find points where I could agree with the general political line.

The state really tried to create equality. We really had equal chances. That might sound strange coming from the daughter of a private craftsman who was discriminated against, but if you proved yourself, you didn't need much money to study or make a career. They kept the rents low. Of course people abused this. The authorities didn't take care of the old houses, and some people stayed in large apartments even though they didn't need them, just because they could afford the rent. There were many families with children who needed the larger apartments. Some people lacked a socialist consciousness. People who were brought up as Christians tended to live the socialist principles more honestly than the socialists did. They were more socialist than the socialists.

I worked as an interpreter for many years and then I had my daughter and decided to get a job which would allow me to spend more time at home. I decided if I was going to have a child, then I wanted to care for her properly. So I got the job at the television station DFF, *Deutscher Fernsehfunk,* where the hours were fixed. I had to be there at 8:00 A.M. and was finished by 5:00. I could also work at home. It was the only TV station and the mouthpiece of the Party, of the government, which made things difficult. Like all the media, they had to do what the people in the Central Committee told them to do. Joachim Hermann was in charge of DFF and he didn't allow the slightest deviation from the Party line.

There were thousands of honest and good Party members at DFF who were opposed to this and had to do things that went against their conscience. It was easier for me because I did freelance work, simultaneous translations of foreign films for editors who then had to decide whether they were suitable for broadcasting. The poor editors had to say: "This American film is good and our people should see it, but there are these sentences which aren't in accordance with our Party line. So we need to make sure during the dubbing that we change them so that the whole film won't be banned by the *Politbüro.*" That was very difficult for the editors, and when they are condemned today by the West German media, it's unjust, because many of them tried hard every day to get a little bit beyond the very rigid Party line, and every millimeter beyond the rigid Party line was a victory. Of course, there were people who took the easy road, which was to obey their superiors, but many tried to save a particular program for the station.

When I first started working there things were very simple: the line was strict and we knew exactly what was allowed. For example, we couldn't show any uniforms, not even forest service uniforms, but this was silly, so eventually we did. Obviously nothing anti-communist was allowed. I remember there was one year when there were no candles in the shops. We simply could not get any candles, and it was Christmas. We had to view all the films and cut the candles out. Our announcers had Christmas decorations on their desks, but there were no candles in them. They didn't want the people to say, "They've got candles, why don't we." Then there was the time we had to cut out all gorgeous meals. It was simply silly.

In September 1989 I gave up my job as a translator and became an editor because my daughter had turned fifteen and wasn't home much. I had separated from my second husband, and it was very lonely at home. The first production I had to deal with as an editor was a film called *Christofo Columbo*, a joint production of France, Italy, and the United States, I think, and there was a sequence where Columbus's dying wife said to him: "For all the years we've been married you've dreamed of finding this magnificent country in the West. You must try to find it." In the second part of the film the sailors complained that Columbus never went south, never went north, he always went west. This was at the time when thousands of people were leaving for the West, and the line would have been a huge joke for our viewers, but we simply could not allow the country to have their laugh. The Party would have been against it. It was ridiculous because Columbus did go west. We decided to keep the sequence in the film and wait and see how the mood was on the day of the telecast. If the mood was strict, we would cut the sequence. Given the system we were forced to work within, it was a kind of a victory to leave it in and see whether the political viewers would notice it. But the *Wende* came and we didn't have to cut it. Now we don't have to do this ridiculous editing anymore.

I don't think that DFF had a very great influence on people before the *Wende* because most of the people didn't watch it. They watched West German stations. After listening to socialist propaganda all day at work they didn't want to have to hear it on TV too. That wasn't very realistic or very just, but it's the way things were. I watched DFF a lot because over the years it became more and more interesting and more varied even than the West German stations. But of course I also watched West German television.

After the *Wende* we got rid of the big Party hard-liners first, but no one was willing to take the positions of responsibility and to work full hours. There were some people in my department, people in the Party whom I respected, the courageous ones, who did accept positions of responsibility. I never was interested because as a single parent I have lots of responsibilities at home and I simply don't have time to be a big boss. A big boss always has somebody at home doing the household chores and taking care of the children.

Things got easier for us at the station. After the monetary union we no longer had the problem of hard currency, and we could buy whatever we could afford. But after unification many people lost their jobs. Whoever left on holiday after May 1990 called the office to find out whether they should bother to come back to work the next Monday. First they got rid of people near retirement age, but that wasn't enough. Then the department directors were instructed to fire 30 percent of their personnel, regardless of the work to be done. First they fired the people who had been recently hired. But that wasn't enough, so then they announced there would be another wave of two thousand, only they weren't going to announce them before Christmas because the suicide rate would be too high. It was unbearable. We went to work and didn't know what our colleagues were doing behind our backs to convince our bosses that we should be fired. They tried to avoid firing single women with children, but it was unavoidable. They didn't follow a "ladies first" principle because the majority of the people working in television were women. In our editorial office there were five men and twenty women.

I must admit that the level of productivity in my department was amazingly low. It's true that there were places at DFF where the work could have been done with fewer people, but I don't like the West Germans' saying that we're all lazy and we don't know how to work. The reason why there were so many people working in some areas and so few in others had to do with the pay system, a system that simply didn't work. There were people needed in places where there were a lot of jobs but the pay was so low people simply didn't want to work there. Productivity should have been balanced better.

For as long as it lasts, DFF is trying to meet the needs of East Germans. They're in the same boat and can identify with the people. The West German stations have their propaganda and their pre-formed images of us, as we have for many aspects of West German life. Of course we watched West German television and were interested in that paradise across the border. I think our ideas about West Germany are more realistic than the ideas the West Germans have about us. When you watch talk shows, for example, it's clear that the people from the West and the people from the East want to talk to each other, to explain things. But it's impossible. As soon as an *Ossi* tries to say something, the *Wessi* replies with the pre-formed image they have gotten from their media.

During the summer of 1989 I was very depressed when I heard about all the young people who were leaving the country. The West German television stations really stirred things up through their coverage, and our Party leadership kept silent. Every morning I looked for some response to the situation in the newspaper, but the Party was acting as though nothing were happening. Then came October 7 and the fortieth anniversary of the GDR. Everybody knew that something was going to happen. There was a big FDJ march with torches and Gorbachev was going to be there. My daughter wanted to go. She was very enthusiastic—she loved her GDR. I let her because I thought she was intelligent enough to find out the truth step by step by herself. But on that night I did something I'd never done before: I forbade her to go to the march, not because I was against the march, but because I was afraid she might get hurt in a riot. She was furious with me. She watched the march on TV and was very sad.

We had great hopes for change. The greatest day was November 4 at Alexanderplatz when thousands of people gathered. That was proof to me that the new government was serious about change. The speeches that were given there would never have been allowed even a few weeks before. Krenz gave a speech, Markus Wolf, Stefan Heym, and Christa Wolf. This was absolutely new for us. It was broadcast live on television, the first live broadcast ever in the GDR. Of course the Party congresses were also broadcast live, but they were carefully prepared and can't be compared with November 4. I wasn't at the demonstration because my daughter wouldn't let me go; this was her revenge. She said, "No Mommy, I'm afraid there might be a riot." I took it calmly, and we watched the whole thing on TV, which was actually better because you could hear the speeches much more clearly. Markus Wolf was deputy minister for state security for a long time, and when he spoke there was shouting and whistling, and I thought that the counterrevolution was about to begin. I was really afraid. I couldn't believe what was happening. It was the greatest day.

On November 9 I saw the press conference on television when Günther Schabowski said they were going to allow people to go to the West, but I didn't understand what it meant. I thought he was saying they were going to ease travel restrictions, that's all. One journalist became famous for saying, "Whoever is asleep on this night must be dead." The next morning after we found out what had happened I told my daughter that I didn't approve. I thought there would be great chaos as there was in 1961, and I was sad. We didn't go to the Ku'Damm with the thousands because I felt ashamed that people were behaving like poor starving *Ossis,* gratefully accepting a free glass of beer. Other people said that the friendliness was wonderful, the joy. We went to West Berlin later, but we didn't have much money, and I didn't like the feeling that I was a beggar. Both my daughter and I had picked up our DM 100, the "welcome money" that the West German government had been giving every GDR citizen on her first visit to the West for the last three years. Why shouldn't we? We each bought a nice bag for DM 50 and the other DM 50 we saved for a trip to England. All those years I studied English I hadn't been allowed to go to England. One day we will have enough money saved.

I'm as much a leftist now as I was before the *Wende.* The difference is that the attitude I had before the *Wende* was considered by the hard-liners to be reactionary, and now any shade of red is considered Stalinist. Again there is a stamp on it. My attitude hasn't changed: I still oppose people who simply echo the state policy without thinking for themselves. I think that the principles of Marxism are correct, as I believe in the principles of Christianity. Many of the things we learned in Marxist-Leninist instruction and which we groaned about then can be observed now, for example, how capitalism works. What they're doing with the GDR now is the enactment of the basic principle of colonization. It's like the textbook I had to read in the 1960s.

I was also branded by the SED regime. First I was branded the daughter of an exploiter. Then I studied English literature at the university, which meant that I was seen as reactionary. The people who studied Russian literature were the progressives. Because my mother had taught me to say "thank you" and "please," I was branded bourgeois because at that time bourgeois manners were considered unsocialist. As a freelance worker I was an SED outcast for many years until I could prove I was a reliable person. For all those years I was stamped.

Now people are stamping people in the other direction. I have to be very careful at work. Some friends warned me not to express my sympathy for the PDS and [PDS head] Gregor Gysi or to criticize what's happening now. If I say that someone who was in the Party for forty years is a decent person I get stamped as a Stalinist. People do not differentiate. Again they are following the party line, only this time it's the CDU line. The people who were in the SED for the sake of their career conformed to the Party line because it was demanded of them. Now a positive attitude toward the market economy is demanded, and they are supplying it. I think that human beings adapt to any situation—that's all. It's not a matter of believing, it's a matter of adapting to what's required. That's why so many people can change so quickly.

I didn't have to change. I was a Christian, very opposed to the state, even to the point where I wanted to commit suicide because I couldn't bear it any longer. But then I remembered that Thomas Mann had once said you can't live your life in constant opposition, so I tried to have a positive but critical attitude toward this country. As a freelancer I didn't have to do a lot of things, such as attend Party meetings, so I was lucky. I could support the larger philosophy but I wasn't subjected to the many tiny things that made life difficult for people.

I'm not a member of the PDS, and I don't know whether I will ever join a party, but I sympathsize with the PDS because I like Gregor Gysi very much and I respect the PDS's efforts to maintain the good in Marxism and to criticize the bad things Marxism did in the past. No other party here is doing that. The Christian Democrats in the GDR were simply swallowed by the Christian Democrats in West Germany, and they aren't about to criticize themselves. The *Ossis* hardly have a role within the newly combined CDU.

I don't think that the FRG is an ideal country. What I don't like is their arrogance, and they treat us and everything in the GDR with arrogance. I never wanted to be a citizen of the FRG, and now I've been made one. I wanted to stay in the GDR and try to improve things. Maybe if we had taken our time during the Modrow government, we could have looked around Europe and found some models we liked better, perhaps Sweden or Austria. Austria is a small country with very good relations with the FRG and a system similar to the West German system, but they are not the same country. Again we are subject to unknown forces. Again we know what's wrong, just as we did during the SED regime, but we can't do anything about it.

July 1992

Gerda Maron was deeply disappointed with life in the new united Germany. She saw the increasingly obvious obsession with money as a fundamental loss and was searching for some values to provide a sense of security in what she perceived as an ever changing society. She noted, "The real problem is that there are no non-material values to teach your children." An additional source of frustration was the lack of challenge in her new job. In West Berlin she worked at the British Council, answering the telephone and sorting the mail, and although she was making a respectable salary and using her language skills, she resented doing work that was so far below what she was qualified to do.

During the interview I was struck by her extensive collection of newspaper articles dealing with the Wende *which she brought out to illustrate and augment her comments. Fascinated with the new but not ready to give up the old, Gerda Maron refused to be caught up in the frenzy to buy a Western automobile. She was proud to say, "I still have my Wartburg, and I plan to keep it."*

Ursula Korth,

forty-seven, import-export office,

East German Television (DFF)

February 1991

Ursula Korth was moved to tears when the Wall opened, thankful to the young people who had gone into the streets to demonstrate for reform. Although she herself had not demonstrated, she had witnessed the police violence surrounding the fortieth anniversary of the GDR on October 7, 1989, and had tried to intervene when several police roughed up a young man on the street near her apartment. Wanting to thank these young people, she voted for New Forum in the March 18 elections. However, when she realized that many of the ideas of New Forum were too idealistic to become reality, she voted for the CDU. She said a vote for CDU was a vote for unification.

Ursula Korth remembered the days when she had had to struggle to make ends meet, having raised a child alone before the policies that eased the burden for single mothers had been put into place. "I never believed in the ideal of socialism," she said. "What they told us had nothing to do with reality. . . . I somehow never felt emotionally connected to it all."

With the dissolution of East German television she knew that the job she had held for twenty-four years would disappear. She dreaded the thought of welfare but was far from despondent. She made it clear that loss of job security was small in comparison to the new freedom she had gained.

Ursula Korth

On the night of November 9, the night the Wall came down, I was lying in bed watching the late news, and suddenly I saw people going down the Born-holmerstrasse, about a half kilometer from here, and crossing over the border.

They were greeted on the other side by West Berliners with champagne bottles. I lay here in my bed and cried. I really cried. People were interviewed as they crossed, and the ones in my age group who experienced the building of the Wall were also in tears. People were overwhelmed that what had been forbidden for so many years was suddenly possible within a few hours. I saw men crying like babies. I wasn't crying out of disappointment over the lost years. I was crying because I was thankful for the people who had had the courage to go out into the streets in the weeks before—the young people.

For example, on October 8, I heard the news that young people who had demonstrated in the Schönhauser Allee had been met by police. Since we often got differing news reports from the East and West media, I decided to go have a look for myself. I took the subway just one station to Schönhauser Allee and, sure enough, there were the police. They stood two or three rows deep and blocked one of the exits. So I went out the other side and saw soldiers, police cars, and police with dogs—all blocking the street. They also had trucks with snow plows attached to the front to plow the people away. The young people stood on the street and yelled, "No violence!" But I could only hear this—I couldn't see them because the police blocked the view.

I wanted to walk back home and had to take side streets because I couldn't get through Schönhauser Allee. I saw a young man being pulled out of his car. Somehow he had gotten through the police blockade, and even though he hadn't hurt anyone, he was dragged out of his car and slammed against the side of it, the way you see in police movies. They accused him of running over someone. A young man and I stood and watched for a while, and when we saw that they weren't about to let go and things were getting serious, we went up to the policemen and said we wanted to see the person who had been run over. Of course, there was no one there. So we gave the young man our names and addresses and told him that he could use us as witnesses if necessary.

He was charged with assault against the state forces. I thought they would let him go after they cooled down a bit, but then a few days later, a detective came here and asked me to come make a statement. They had in fact arrested him, as they did so many others that night. I was a little afraid, but I went down to the police and gave my statement. I felt I had to because it was a matter of justice. I never saw the young man again. Not too long after the *Wende* I called the police to find out what had happened to him, and I was told that he had been released. I didn't know what was going to happen next. I didn't know that very soon there would be no more violence at all.

I come from a family that wasn't suited for this state. It was only by chance that they lived in the eastern part of the country, and they weren't communists. I was never in the Young Pioneers or the FDJ. Back then you didn't necessarily get penalized for not joining; later it was unimaginable not to join. Of course I was never in the Party. I somehow never felt emotionally connected to it all. I experienced how they walled us in in 1961 and suffered tremendously as a result. I was seventeen years old then; life was just beginning. I had finished my training and was ready to see the world, and they simply closed it up. I worked near the border and saw the Wall grow from day to day. On the first day I thought, no, this is impossible, they won't be able to keep this up, you can't divide an entire city and an entire country. But they did, and things kept getting worse.

In the early seventies I became involved with a man from Iraq. I experienced firsthand what the divided city really meant—he lived in West Berlin and I lived in East Berlin. I was working for the television station, which belonged to the state apparatus. Everyone working there was forbidden to have any contacts with the people in the West. So it had to be secret. All my mail was opened, every package. It was a terrible feeling. I never knew who would be the first to read my letters and always had to decide whether I should write about what was important to me or not. This was not the freedom they had told us about. I never believed in the ideal of socialism. What they told us had nothing to do with reality.

For twenty-four years I worked for the state-run television station, DFF. I dealt with the buying and selling of films, import-export. I was trained as a secretary and never had time to go to college because of my son. I was also more interested in practical work. I never got married, but I thought it was important to have a child, and I've never regretted it. But it wasn't as simple as it's made out to be. Even though I was a single mother my son wasn't taken into day care—there wasn't a place for him. Of course I had to work—back then we only got three months maternity leave. On paper I had the right to a space at a *Kinderkrippe*, but I didn't get it. There weren't enough places for everyone, and you had to have connections. That was 1969. Later I got my son into day care.

When I started working at DFF in 1967, it wasn't such a big deal if I wasn't in the Party. I said I wasn't mature enough. They finally noticed that there was no point. They didn't make things particularly difficult for me, but I never had a chance to move up. I was allowed to work there, but I would never have been considered for a management position. I wouldn't have wanted to have such a position anyway because it would have required extra work and many extra meetings that I had no interest in.

I was also asked whether I wanted to work for the Stasi. I had applied to work at a place that dealt with foreigners, so they asked me if I would be willing to give information. I withdrew my application. Everyone watched everyone else. Also at work. I stated my opinions anyway. One time they refused to grant me a visa to go to Hungary. I complained. I'm sure there is a small Stasi file on me somewhere. There's a lot of talk about people who worked for the Stasi, but you never know how they were recruited. For example, Bärbel Bohley, who I met briefly when I was involved with New Forum, explained on TV that she was spied on for years by one of her best friends. This woman had been raised in a children's home and thought she owed it to the state that had raised her to keep an eye on her good friend. She never thought she was doing anything wrong.

In the first free *Volkskammer* elections on March 18, I voted for Coalition 90/ New Forum because they were the ones who got most involved with the whole Stasi question. After that first election I didn't vote for New Forum anymore. I voted for CDU because I realized that the ideas of New Forum were too far removed from reality, and everything was going in the direction of unification. A vote for CDU meant a vote for unification. Not that I liked very many of the CDU people who were in the old GDR block party CDU.

I feel much better personally with the *Wende* and unification. I certainly feel freer. I'm not afraid of saying something wrong. There aren't so many meetings at work. Now we work 40 hours per week instead of 43¾. Everything is less complicated. The most important thing is to keep my job. I can't imagine living on welfare or unemployment compensation. But I know that by the end of the year I'll be out of work. The whole TV station is being dissolved.

Still I'm optimistic. I have to be. Last summer I almost found out what unemployment meant. I verbally attacked someone at work because I thought he worked for the Stasi. That turned out not to be a very good idea of mine. So I quit because I thought I would have lots of problems. For about two weeks I tried to find another job, but it was impossible. Thank goodness I was able to get rehired at the TV station. But the uncertainty was terrible. The Stasi guy left and is now in Cologne. I still don't know if I was right to do what I did.

There were lots of people with privileges who felt right at home in this state and didn't want unification, but I was very happy about unification. I always felt like a second-class citizen when we were in Czechoslovakia or Hungary. Our money couldn't buy anything in comparison to the West Germans who we ran into there all the time. We wondered why there was such a great difference. We worked hard too, and they weren't any smarter than we were. So I was very happy about the *Wende*, especially for my son. My son can now travel where he wants. I never even considered leaving the GDR when the Hungarian border opened. I was too old to think about starting over. I feel at home here, in spite of the problems and the difficulties I had and am having still. I prefer to live here with the contradictions. I had to live with them for many years.

July 1992

The East German television station DFF was indeed dissolved, but Ursula Korth was hired into a similar position at the newly formed radio and television station in Brandenburg (Ostdeutscher Rundfunk Brandenburg, ORB). *She said that she was well paid but was working so hard that she had no time for her private life. She did not like the new one-hour commute to work but made it clear that she was not complaining. She was tired of hearing all the whining, she said.*

Reflecting upon our first interview, she said so much had happened in the meantime that the opening of the Wall had simply been forgotten. She missed nothing of the GDR but feared the increased street violence which had already touched her family: her son had been beaten on the street by young thugs. As I was leaving, she gave me her son's copy of The Meaning of Our Lives (Vom Sinn unseres Lebens), *the book GDR children were given at age fourteen on the occasion of their* Jugendweihe, *the Party's secular equivalent to confirmation. When I protested that her son might want to keep it as a memento of his past, he came out of his room and assured me that he had no use for it.*

Marianne S.,

twenty, language student at
Humboldt University

February 1991

Marianne's interview is testimony to the daily intrusion by the state into the lives of its youngest citizens. In day care she was required to draw a tank to honor People's Army Day. Later she knew that joining the FDJ was necessary if she hoped to have any future at the university. "You accepted this GDR identity without thinking about it," she commented. The discrepancy between what young people were told and what they experienced—when visitors came from the West, for example—caused considerable confusion. This discrepancy was so great that GDR youth, according to Marianne, stopped believing anything they were told. She claims, "We were fed the friendship with the Soviet Union, and then fatherland GDR, and finally father Honecker."

However, the educational system appeared to be successful in inculcating the notion of loyalty to the SED-state in many of its pupils. In contrast to the People's Republic of China, where students were the moving force behind the demonstrations in Tiananmen Square in July 1989, students were not highly visible in the streets of Leipzig, Dresden, or East Berlin later that year. The university was "the place where ideology was disseminated." In addition, students knew they were being watched by members of the state security on the university teaching staff. Marianne's department, which prepared foreign language students for careers as interpreters, was observed particularly closely because its graduates would become members of the elite Reisekader, those who were allowed to travel to the West. Beyond that, there was a high level of distrust even among the students themselves. She saw no reason to engage in political activities which could ruin her hopes for a career. Marianne wanted to leave Germany altogether when she finished her university degree, finding a place where she might be able to forge a new identity and come to terms with her uncomfortable GDR *past.*

Marianne S.

The *Wende* was very dramatic for my family. Before that I never knew who my father was. My mother never told me. After the *Wende* I went to my mother and said, "Mom, now that things have changed it's time that you told me about my father." So she did. It turns out that he was a Westerner she had had an affair with. She was never able to breathe a word about him. When I took my entrance exam for the university they asked me if I could tell them whether my father was in the Party. How could I tell them whether he was in the Party if I didn't even know who he was?

I knew other children who lived alone with their mothers, but in these other cases the mothers were divorced from the fathers. I think these kids missed their fathers more than I did, since I never knew mine. I never felt any discrimination or any negative attitude from other kids because I didn't have a father. When my mother went on business trips I stayed with friends of my mother's who had kids my age. I couldn't go to *Kinderkrippe* because I had chronic ear infections, so my grandmother took me during the day until I was three and old enough to go to day care. It was attached to the factory, and since I spent all my time there, I didn't have any playmates at home. I had to leave home at 7:00 in the morning and got home at 6:00 in the evening. I don't have any bad memories of day care, except that there was this distinction between children who had toys from the West and kids who didn't. Sometimes we had a day where all the kids were supposed to bring their favorite toy. The day care worker would single out one child and say, "That's the nicest toy. I like that the best." For a small child who has brought her nicest teddy bear or nicest doll, that is terrible. You could see yourself that the Barbie doll was nicer than our dolls, but when you only had one of our dolls, you didn't notice that it wasn't so nice.

Later I was in the state youth organization, the FDJ. Membership wasn't required, but if you wanted to get your high school diploma and go on to the university, you had to be in the FDJ. You didn't have to kill yourself participating in activities, but you needed to have organized some afternoon event or something. It didn't have to be political. There was a meeting once a month for all members where the events were evaluated or something like that. At our school, these meetings died out over the course of the year because gradually fewer and fewer kids attended. The meetings were simply too boring. There was always a part of the meeting devoted to political discussion where someone read an article from the newspaper or something, which for students in the tenth grade was not very interesting or challenging. If I'm interested in politics then I've already read the paper, and if I'm not interested in politics, this isn't going to get me interested. The FDJ-sponsored activities were similar to the activities that the youth groups in the West had: discos, hobby afternoons where someone demonstrated sewing, for example, or readings by authors. I enjoyed some of the events and never felt they were a burden. There was a required program that you had to complete every month, including these monthly meetings, and then there were the voluntary activities for those who were interested. We tried to get away from the political stuff and sometimes just closed our eyes. It didn't matter to us whether a class field trip was organized by the FDJ or not. We simply didn't pay any attention whether an FDJ flag hung over the entrance or whether a picture of Erich Honecker was in the cafeteria. If there was a picture, we just didn't look at it.

When I was finishing up my high school diploma they started recruiting me for the Party. You could become a Party member at age eighteen. Teachers who everyone knew were in the Party took me aside and invited me to a Party meeting. One thing that got me about these meetings was that we had to use the informal "du" with the teachers, because Party members always used "du" with each other. Then the next day at school you had to use the formal "Sie" again. That was a weird situation. I told them that I wanted more time to think about it. It was too early for me to make a decision; I was much too young. Besides I wanted to make something of myself first. Then I could tell them my experience had shown me that what they were doing was right.

The Party recruiters didn't go after me. They presented the idea to us and we could attend meetings. Then we would become "candidates" for a year, which meant we didn't have to pay Party dues, and they could see if we were worthy. If we said no, that was the end of it. We weren't harassed or anything like that. Most of the teachers were Party members, and the ones that weren't kept silent about it. It wasn't a major topic of discussion at school because most of the teachers didn't wear their Party buttons. Men were supposed to wear them on their suits all the time, but women were relieved of the duty because they couldn't stick them on their blouses very well. Some people even wore them to the theater because they thought they might run into a Party official. I thought it was abnormal to press people into something like that. If I have certain convictions, I have them whether or not I wear my button. There were many things here that served to create an exterior image. None of my close friends joined the Party. We all refused to embrace the Party because we didn't have any others to choose from.

Of course there were some kids who were convinced socialists. I knew two. One girl never looked to the right or to the left and thought that the Party was always right—even as late as last year. She's at the university with me, and the *Wende* was almost tragic for her. She just stood there and said, "They always told us it was good." The other girl liked the idea of socialism, and the idea isn't bad, only she thought it needed reform. Most of the kids I knew were against the system, although only a small minority were outspoken about it. Some kids took their protest in the wrong direction. I know a guy who joined the Skinhead movement because he wanted to rebel at any cost. He said he couldn't stand things any more. I don't think that's a very good way to fight the system. But most kids didn't do much because everyone knew they wouldn't be admitted to the university if they created too many problems. Sometimes there were events where we were allowed to voice our opinion, but someone always sat in the back and took notes, and that information made its way into a report. There was an inner timidity and, in a way, a deadening to the political stuff. At some point you simply said, okay, why should I martyr myself here, I want to build a future for myself. And then you didn't know exactly what to believe and thought that the things you heard from the West perhaps really were all propaganda, and things here really weren't so bad.

After I got my high school diploma I wanted to work as a hotel receptionist, but you had to have connections to get a job in a good hotel, and I didn't have any. The only other possible training positions for me would have been hairdresser, waitress, or saleswoman. There was no such thing as foreign language secretary here in the GDR. You were a secretary and if you were really good you learned foreign languages on the side. So I decided to start at the university and get my degree as an interpreter. Maybe by then the job market would have become somewhat more normal. I couldn't even get a position in a training program right now, it's that bad. A friend of mine tried to get accepted into a training program that only requires the tenth grade, and she has her high school diploma, and there was nothing, absolutely nothing.

I thought the *Wende* was good, but we should have been able to democratize ourselves alone. The whole unification thing moved much too fast. We should have had time to reach the economic level of the West and then come together. Now we have the feeling that we're not accepted anywhere. I went to the Employment Office in West Berlin today to look for a vacation job because my present job as a salesperson at a department store didn't turn out to be what they promised—instead of two months full time it turns out to be "when needed." So I went to the Employment Office. They were encouraging and told me they were looking for students—until they found out I was from East Berlin. Then they said, "Why don't you try your own Employment Office first?" The West Berlin Employment Office knows that there are so many more pressing cases here in East Berlin that the office can't be bothered with students who want a job during the vacation. I'm sad that nothing will remain of what we had. The FRG bureaucracy, which I've come in contact with through my financial aid application, is twice as bad as ours, and we always complained about ours.

When I traveled I found myself confronted with my identity as a citizen of the GDR. I didn't like those West Germans whose attitude was, "Here we are and how much does the world cost; we can afford it." When they were abroad, some East Germans tried to imitate this arrogant behavior which disgusted me. I've gotten to know some students from West Berlin and they don't make me feel inferior. I took a trip to Paris for two weeks and all the French people I met asked me why we had allowed ourselves to be annexed like this. Why were we letting them treat us so badly? Didn't we have any backbone? I couldn't explain it to them; they don't know how things were here.

I was always against things that were forced on me, and from childhood on we were fed the GDR identity. That started in day care where we had to draw a tank for People's Army Day, and then we were fed the friendship with the Soviet Union, and then fatherland GDR, and finally father Honecker. The principle was that you accepted this GDR identity without questioning it. This was a big mistake because it was important for people to learn to think for themselves. For example, we always heard that capitalism was foul and dying, and then when grandmother or Aunt Emma came for a visit from the West and showed us what she had brought us, we wondered why—if we had such a flourishing economy—our chocolate didn't taste as good as hers. The discrepancy between what we were told and what we experienced was so great that we stopped believing anything we were told.

I've always had problems with the German mentality. Germans take too much time thinking about things, time they could be using for living. In the

present situation, people I know are making lists of all the negative consequences that could arise if they took a particular job. Then there is the fact
that the Germans still have the feeling they have to be ashamed of their past.
Granted, the German past is not terrific, but people don't still reproach the
French for the fact that Napoleon conquered almost all of Europe, although it's
wrong to compare the Napoleonic wars with World War II. But in the case of
other peoples, they let the past be past. My only crime was having been born in
Germany.

I enjoyed talking with the French about their multicultural population because I had the impression that they are able to handle it better than we are. I
was sitting in a cafe with some French kids together with an Algerian student,
and they all had a wonderful relationship with each other. The Cubans and
Vietnamese who were working here were supposed to work but not go to cafes,
movies, and certainly not the theater. When people from here went to Kreuz-
berg in West Berlin for the first time and saw all the Turks, a lot of them
asked, "How can they allow that?" Others said, "That's great, this multicultural
society."

People really started talking about and noticing the Stasi during the fall of
1989. When so many people started going to Hungary the Stasi started appear-
ing everywhere. I was at the airport because just by chance I was going to
Hungary myself during the summer of 1989, and anyone with a practiced eye
could tell who the Stasi people were: tennis shoes, small umbrella, rain coat.
They were just waiting for someone to say, "I can't wait to get out of here," and
then they would say, "Please come with me, young man, you're not flying
anywhere." In fact lots of strange things began happening. People weren't allowed to fly, or their personal I.D. was somehow lost at the Ministry.

Some friends of mine left the GDR via Hungary. I had been with them in
Bulgaria during the summer. One was working as a waitress in a cafe here in the
Nikolai quarter and when I went to see her she told me she was taking another
vacation. I said, "But you don't have any vacation time left." And she said, "Yes I
do, I'm going to Hungary in three days." I must have looked at her funny,
because she nodded, and then I knew what she was going to do. Of course it was
impossible to discuss it in public, so I never talked with her about it. I was really
sorry because I liked them both and I knew I'd never hear from them again.
She's a waitress and he's a carpenter and they're both young, so they'll probably
be okay. Another guy from my school also left.

I never talked with any of them about why they were leaving, but I can imagine they were tired of working so hard and getting nowhere. And then there was always the feeling of being second-class citizens. When we were all in Bulgaria I noticed that the restaurant doors were opened for Westerners and they were invited to come again, and if you didn't pay in deutsch Marks you got a beach umbrella in the sixth row, far away from the water. There were these little things where you felt you weren't equal. The guy I was with in school was the one who ended up in the Skinhead movement. He said, "I can't stand it here any more, I just want out." He's in West Berlin now, and actually he's not doing so well because he's still fighting the prejudices against us. At work they say, "So, you're from East Berlin. Let's see what you can do." Lots of people here took too seriously what they were told by people in the Western media: "You can all come, and we're happy with everyone who comes." Even within the family, the relatives in the West wrote and sent Christmas packages as long as the Wall stood, and now we don't hear from them because they're terrified their *Ossi* relatives will show up.

I thought about leaving during the summer of 1989 too, and I was in Hungary. But I was with my boyfriend, and he was supposed to start his stint in the army. If you wanted to be admitted to the university you had to spend three years in the army. So there we were in Hungary and we read in the paper that they had opened the Hungarian border. We talked about leaving. But if I had left I would have destroyed my mother's life, and at that point no one could have predicted that things would fall apart so fast. My mother would have been fired immediately. The Stasi would have seen to it that she didn't get another job. For me there was a conflict of conscience. We could have stayed with my boyfriend's relatives in West Berlin, I could have gone to the university there. But I didn't want to be so dependent on other people. With just a high school diploma I wouldn't have been able to find a decent job. There were already lots of East Germans in West Berlin.

But I never felt the presence of the Stasi terribly strongly. I had direct contact with them twice at the university, the first time when they asked me whether my father was in the Party, and the second time at a meeting. We were supposed to talk about what we liked and didn't like in our university program. We were told that this meeting was going to be different and no one would be sitting there taking notes. And then a man sat up front and took notes. They asked us what we thought of this opportunity to express ourselves. Everyone laughed. Then they asked me, and I said, "Actually something like this should build trust but when we're lied to from the beginning there's no point to such a discussion, and there's no need to have another one. If you tell us no one will take notes and then someone does take notes, then you might just as well tell us to write down what we have to say; it would be much easier that way." We sometimes had very incompetent teachers in our last two years of high school and then we assumed that they were from the Stasi because bad teachers usually weren't allowed to teach the college-preparatory courses.

During the fall of 1989 things really began to happen. Friends got together and discussed things. For example, we knew some people who had been beaten during the demonstration on October 7, and we asked them what had really gone on there. Had they really done what we saw on West television? We tried to get accurate information because we heard two completely different news reports. Our media reported almost nothing, or said a few people were demonstrating, and the Western media said how bad everything was, and talked about a police state, and how could they, and so on.

On November 4 I was at the demonstration at Alexanderplatz and was shocked to see the *Drzinsky,* a special unit of the army that was responsible to the Stasi. They had a different uniform than did the regular police. In principle they were the Stasi in uniform. A friend of mine had been drafted into this unit and said, "Marianne, you wouldn't believe how they tell us to behave during demonstrations. They tell us to use our weapons, and we practice one-on-one combat." He was really upset because he knew he would be fighting against his own people. Most of the demonstrators were our age.

Then came November 9. I was watching television that evening and heard them say that anyone who wanted to could leave. I understood that to mean leave permanently. And I thought, sure, those who want to leave can leave. Then people started going over to the border to have a look. A girlfriend of mine called and asked me if I wanted to go with her. That was my first experience of West Berlin. The first thing I wanted to see was the Charlottenburg Palace and the Egyptian Museum with Nefertiti. I asked the first policeman I saw how to get there. Our city maps didn't have West Berlin on them. He looked at me and asked me where I was from. From East Berlin, I said. He was shocked: "What, you don't want to shop?" And I thought, what do they think of us, anyway? Shopping, a few bananas, that was too simple. When we got to Charlottenburg the guard started complaining about the *Ossis,* how they were flooding the Ku'Damm and begging, and then we told him we were from East Berlin ourselves, and he apologized and disappeared.

The university didn't play a very big role in all of this. For one thing, the university was the place where ideology was disseminated and, for another, we had a number of professors who we knew worked for the Stasi. Our department was watched particularly closely because it educated the interpreters who then traveled outside the country, the so-called *Reisekader*. In addition I knew if I stood up and said that things weren't right, I would be the one not to get a job and then I wouldn't be able to change anything anyway. I would lose everything and gain nothing. No one knew exactly how broad the opposition movement was. I didn't know who I could talk to or who I could depend on to support me in public. Everyone agreed with you when you were talking in the cafeteria, but if you said something in any sort of public forum, people said, "Yeah, well, sure, everything has two sides."

As a woman I never felt as equal as the propaganda said I should. For a while I thought I wanted to go into a training program dealing with foreign trade and I was told that men are tougher negotiaters than women, and I wasn't admitted to the program. Then I went to the College of Economics to an advising session and was told, "If you want to study foreign trade I'm sorry we have no room for you." The woman tried to persuade me to go into military economics where I could become an officer, wear a nice uniform, and wouldn't have to worry about anything. I was really angry, because I knew that with my grades they would have taken me if I had been a boy. Then when I was admitted to the last two years of high school, the EOS, I was told up front that if a girl had an A— average and a boy had a B+, they would take the boy with the B+.

Now women are becoming much more dependent on men. Before, a woman could support herself plus two or three children, and now this is slipping backward, which is too bad. Maybe it's good to say that day care isn't the be-all and the end-all and the mother should take care of her own child, but, if a mother wants to work, she should have the opportunity to do that. It's very sad that our day care facilities are being closed or are on the brink of bankruptcy because they're no longer being subsidized. For me personally, I would consider having a child without a husband, as my mother did. But now it's much more difficult. My mother was able to take me to day care, but that opportunity may not exist for me.

I'm not the type of person to get depressed. I have been furious about what's been happening to us here, but since I can't change it, I have to accept it. When I'm finished with my studies I'd like to leave Germany altogether. I'll see how the job market develops. I've started taking courses at the university in teaching German as a foreign language so that I can teach German outside Germany. My mother doesn't know what she'll do. She knows she doesn't want to go to West Germany; it's the same mentality. If she were to leave, it would probably be for the rest of her life.

Next week I'm going to try to visit my father. First I might just look at him from a distance and then decide whether I want to get any closer. Maybe he'll be very rich and walk around with his nose in the air and I won't exactly feel like going up to him and saying, "Can you remember a little incident twenty years ago?" I'd like to get together and talk, but I'm not sure how I'm going to go about it. My mother said it's up to me. She said it's my right. That's all she said.

July 1992

Soon after our first conversation, Marianne took advantage of the new freedom to travel and went to London to study English and marketing. She loved London and appreciated being able to do what had been denied to many before her: to study English in a country where it was spoken. Upon her return she noticed that the pace of real unification was shockingly slow. Friends of hers had gone West for apprenticeships, and she worried whether they would come back. "Unification was supposed to keep them here, wasn't it?"

Also troubling was the increase in right wing extremism which made her feel unsafe walking around Alexanderplatz at night. Still she was more comfortable in the eastern part of the city than "on the other side." Contributing to her discomfort with West Germans was her experience at a sales job in West Berlin where she and other young people from Humboldt University had been met with mistrust. "Are you sure you can do this?" they were asked. Even more insulting, their belongings were searched before leaving work to make sure they hadn't stolen anything. "The prejudices are still very strong," she said. "It will take a long time."

Nevertheless Marianne was visibly buoyant. She was not worried about the inability to plan for the future. In fact she was delighted with what she called the new range of possibilities. She seemed older and more self-confident than when we first met.

Gitta Nickel,
fifty-four, filmmaker

March 1991

Gitta Nickel lived in Kleinmachnow, a town just across the border from West Berlin-Zehlendorf. Before World War II Kleinmachnow had been a stronghold of communism, and this tradition continued during the forty years of the GDR with a disproportionately high number of Party functionaries among its residents. Gitta Nickel lived among them in a roomy two-story house with lovely Persian carpets on the hardwood floors and Japanese prints on the walls.

Despite her reputation among some younger GDR filmmakers as a Party loyalist, Gitta Nickel saw herself as a reformer. She also protested the tendency in the West to see the East Germans in monolithic terms. She read the society "like a seismograph," she said, and attempted to show critical situations in her films, such as the way farmers defended themselves against unwelcome changes imposed by the state. She spoke of the courage needed to make these films: only a few of the DEFA filmmakers were willing to take the risks involved. She acknowledged, however, that she was also used by the state. Artists and intellectuals were required "to perform" in order to create a public face for the GDR, and if they performed well, they were rewarded. Gitta Nickel's apparent rewards included, in addition to prizes for her films, trips to western Europe and Japan.

Life histories like Gitta Nickel's call to mind the criticisms in the West German press launched after the Wende *against East German intellectuals who, in the eyes of the West, lacked the courage to openly criticize the state, thereby colluding with it. What critics in the West saw as compliance with the state, however, Gitta Nickel saw as doing the best one could in a difficult situation. She maintained that she had tried to bring reform to the system in a way that would not disrupt the delicate balance between making films and being silenced.*

Even with her strong belief in the principles of socialism, Gitta Nickel was happy to see the dismantling of the Wall, which had run a few hundred meters from her front door step, and she welcomed the new opportunity for increased initiative. At the same time, she was extremely critical of the way in which unification had been forged and doubted whether the people of her generation would ever become "Federal Republic Germans."

Gitta Nickel

I was born in a village forty kilometers from Danzig in what was formerly East Prussia, now part of Poland. My father had a dairy farm, and my mother was a housewife. They had three children, and I lived in an intact, safe world. We lived in the rhythm of the seasons, in contact with nature. I always had a close relationship with people who work the land, and I've made several films about farmers. I have wonderful childhood memories which are connected with certain smells: the smell of freshly baked cake on Saturdays, the smell of floors scrubbed white. Christmas was a magical time with lots of baking, and for us children it was a time filled with excitement. Life was peaceful and upright. We didn't have a luxurious life, but we lived with animals and with nature. Everything was ordered: solid family relationships, solid love relationships. Children were important: we were the next generation, and we were protected.

Then came 1945, and everything was changed. My father hadn't been drafted. He had to stay at home and make sure that milk was produced from all the neighboring dairies. So in 1945 my mother drove us children away from the advancing Russians in a tractor, which was almost impossible with the streets jammed with people. Two French soldiers who had been prisoners of war and had worked in the village actually saved our lives. They got us as far as Danzig. There were other refugees on our tractor with us. One of them was an estate owner. I'll never forget the image of this very old, very rich woman. In her left hand she had a bag of silver and in her right hand a bag of gold, cutlery and things like that. I don't remember who else was there with us. When we got to Danzig a truck took us to a town near Berlin where we had relatives.

Years later I became a German teacher, but I didn't like teaching much. I had always been involved in theater productions at school and at the university, and I wanted to be an actor. Somehow I ended up in Babelsberg where I got to know some film people. I had no idea what was in store for me. The thought of being a film director never entered my mind, but I went to the DEFA film studio and

said, "There's only one thing for me in this life: I want to make children's films."
The DEFA director gave me a position as an unpaid assistant, but soon I was
making feature films as a paid assistant with such great directors as Konrad
Wolf and Ralf Kirsten.

It turned out that I was better suited to real-life films than to fiction, and I
worked for quite a while with a documentary film director. Then in 1965 I made
my first films which dealt with German–Soviet relations. The first was about
German and Russian children learning each other's language by playing together. It won a prize at the Moscow film festival. Very quickly I began to devote
myself to women's issues in my films. I made a number of films about women
and also about socialism—this society, this country—including the most varied
subject areas, but always including the role of women in society.

The image of the filmmaker who was loyal to the Party is very superficial. It
was not necessary to be in the Party if you wanted to be in the media. That
image is very one-sided, undifferentiated. Of course there were people who
were loyal to the Party, very ideological, but a lot of them were less doctrinaire.
There wasn't just black and white. That's stupid. It would be dishonest if I didn't
say I felt obligated to this country in a positive way. We believed in this country
to a certain extent. We believed that we could build this socialism; we hoped we
could. We weren't naive either. Even today the idea of socialism isn't bad, even if
it failed in all countries where it was tried. In my opinion, the chance for
creating a decent socialist state on German ground has been lost for the next
century.

I can only speak for myself, but I had honest intentions. I went to school
here, and I never had the feeling that I was fanaticized in any way. I would never
have allowed that sort of thing. We had enough good common sense not to let
ourselves be manipulated. Of course there were tragedies, of course there were
battles, of course there were failures, of course I had to fight terribly to get my
films made, of course some films couldn't be shown for years and years. In spite
of all this, I have to say, I was also very successful. When people see things in
such an undifferentiated way, they say, "She was successful, she must have
agreed with the entire political system. She must have constantly been a cheer-
leader for the political ideology." That's ridiculous! The opposite is true.

Sometimes my films didn't get through the committees, and that was the end
of it, and sometimes my films were put away for two or three years or longer. Of
course I sometimes was afraid, and sometimes I held back. I was sometimes
stronger, sometimes weaker. It was a constant process. Sometimes my films

were direct, and when the political situation was very complicated, I held back and veiled my language.

If I had to qualify what I just said, it would be to say that artists and intellectuals had to perform. In the years when the GDR was fighting for international recognition, we were the ambassadors. They let us travel. They let someone like conductor Kurt Masur travel, great actors and writers, and they gave them in some cases a great deal of license to say and do what they wanted. Sometimes we didn't notice that they were using us, or misusing us at the same time. But if you were good, you didn't have to let them misuse you so much. They decorated themselves with us, even though we often didn't even speak the same language. They gave us prizes. For example, I was awarded a national prize, even if it was only a third-class prize and only once. I was a thorn in their side, and I don't think it would have taken very long for me to have had a complete falling out. That would have happened sometime because again and again I tried to step on forbidden territory. Always. There was a certain group at the DEFA who had the courage to push against the boundaries of the permissible. There weren't many. But I can say that we produced documentaries that will last, that we can show with respect, that have to be taken seriously.

I was attracted to the topic of women in my films because I thought that women here could be truly emancipated, which they actually were to a large extent. We had one of the highest divorce rates, which of course has to do with women's economic independence and with their self-confidence. I maintain still, even if the image of the emancipated woman was exaggerated, that there really were emancipated women, even though only two or three women ever made it into top government positions. But there was so much social support that women were free to work if they wanted to. Every woman could work.

There were always women who were showpieces, but I was more interested in the so-called simple woman who might be the director of a collective farm. I asked them about their daily lives, how they had made it so far, what problems they had run into, where society had supported them and where it had been remiss. I don't want to paint too rosy a picture, but I do think that there were many real opportunities for women in the GDR. Women here had a sense of themselves. This same self-confidence gave me the courage to make my films.

I chose a very male career. I admit, there are a whole crowd of women film directors in West Germany, well known names like Margareta von Trotta and Helke Sander. But only a small number of women succeeded in making their way into filmmaking here. In fact, only a small number of women succeeded in getting into male careers in general: there were very few women pilots, very few directors of industry. Of course that had to do with the times and with the fact that women always had other responsibilities and couldn't devote themselves 150 percent to their careers. It's women who bear children, not men. It's women who take care of children, not men. Those are the classic images which we lived with. We didn't have long enough to get beyond them. We only had forty-five years. What are forty-five years for the development of socialism? Capitalism is hundreds of years old.

Of course I wanted to change things with my films, to get people to talk about things. It was only possible to try to change concrete things, concrete ways of doing things, of living within the family and at work, of behaving, of thinking, of wanting, wherever limits were set. I challenged people to have opinions and the courage to assert those opinions, whether it was inside the family or at work or within the society. The final goal was always to change this society to make life in it better. It sounds like a lot of platitudes, but it's true.

I don't want to overestimate the influence of film, but I think I did have the opportunity to get people to change. I traveled with my films and talked about them with people who saw them. In all seventeen districts of the GDR there were film distributors who organized film showings, matinees in factories. There were film clubs. Documentary films became terribly popular because our films showed people their own lives. There was a real tradition of documentary films. People knew the names of the filmmakers and knew that their films were worth seeing, worth discussing, worth being influenced by so that the ideas could be spread. We had an international documentary film festival in Leipzig, also a national documentary film festival.

Even though I feel like I'm diving into an abyss and might never come out, I'm making another film. It's called "Brothers and Sisters in Germany?" with a question mark. It's about two church ministers, one from the East and one from the West, who exchange congregations for a period of time. One is a woman from a tiny village in the GDR, the other a pastor from the industrial area in West Germany, and the two change positions. They actually did this so that they could experience the other reality, and I wanted to make a film about it. So I raised the money for it.

The pastor experiences the tiny village in the former GDR and the woman minister experiences the industrial area in West Germany where unemployment is high, especially among young people. She is confronted by a group of these young people and drawn into a discussion. She's not used to their blunt talk. You can hear the reservations and the prejudices on both sides coming out. Basically it's not possible for the two sides to come together. Not yet. The arrogance on the one side is still much too great. The kids don't understand that there are people here who have a tremendous amount to offer. It will be a very, very, very complicated process, and I only hope that our people here don't give up. I say "our people" although I never liked the term because the government always talked about "our people."

People in the GDR are beginning to understand how idiotic it was to sell ourselves so quickly, to allow a unification that was dictated. Of course lots of people wanted unification but it went too fast and without a concept, and people understand this now. Now they understand their occupation by the *Wessis,* they understand their humiliation, they understand that they are no longer supposed to be anything or anyone, that they don't mean anything anymore. But they don't understand why. They have exactly as much to offer in this unification as the Germans on the other side. They don't have the slick cars, but they worked just as hard and built something in these forty years. They created values which shouldn't be wiped out in a day.

Of course we have to change. We have to be willing to change these hard and fixed structures that we grew up with. The individual is important now. Before everything was prepared and ordered, and people wanted the opportunity to have more initiative. Now they have the chance to take the initiative and a lot of people simply can't.

I wasn't one of those people who went into the streets in the fall of 1989. I wasn't out there waving the banner of freedom. But I wished for and followed certain things with anticipation and with joy. I never thought the Wall would fall so finally, so terminally, so inexorably. I couldn't imagine that. On November 9, I was in a club with one of my films when I suddenly heard that the Wall was open and that we could travel. I couldn't believe it. We drove to Checkpoint Charlie to see if it was true, and it was. I was already familiar with West Germany because I had been to many film festivals and had made films there. I had even been to Japan. But I was happy because I thought we'd begin slowly, step by step, to develop relations with each other. Others thought it was the beginning of the end.

It's too simple to say that I see things pessimistically. I care very much about what happens to our people. The two peoples have simply been slapped together; the unification has yet to occur. I don't think that my generation will ever become Federal Republic Germans. I don't want to, actually. I'm very happy to have experienced this little piece of the GDR. It gave me a lot. Although I distance myself from the criminal aspects of it, the state security, the whole state complex that spied on its citizens, it will take me a long time to take my leave from this GDR, if I can do it at all.

July 1992

In the time that had passed since I first spoke with Gitta Nickel, she had experienced a whirlwind of productive activity. A trip to China resulted in a television documentary about Eva Siao, a Chinese socialist. Three other TV documentaries dealt with eighty years of German filmmaking in Babelsberg, the home of UFA (pre–World War II film studios) and DEFA (GDR film studios); the departure of the Red Army from the GDR; and the establishment of a new television station in the eastern part of Germany. She had two new works in process: one, the story of a woman cabaret singer in Leipzig; the other, a seven-part series on the GDR. With the latter, Gitta Nickel intended an open-ended depiction of diverse life experiences. "The history of the GDR has yet to be worked through," she said. "This film is a step in that direction."

Gitta Nickel had thrown herself into her work in order to move beyond the difficulty of the Wende, *which she characterized as a kind of personal torture. She found little good to say about the new political situation—travel had been possible for her before. What she missed most was her documentary film studio at DEFA; what she disliked most was an unfamiliar authority—the new market economy— which again limited her creative voice but in a different way than before: "I was told what to do in the GDR, but I knew how to oppose it. That's not the case now."*

Eva P.,

fifty-three, formerly secretary with the Protestant church, now cleans homes

March 1991

In contrast to a number of the women I spoke with, Eva P. was not a consciously political person. She was not in the Party, nor was she a member of the opposition. She worked to hold her family together, not to bring about social change. Nevertheless, her story is political—if in ways that differ substantially from those of intellectuals and opposition activists. Although she did not gather signatures to protest government actions or attend meetings of New Forum, her life reflects the ways in which all GDR *citizens were confronted with political choices on a daily basis.*

Eva P. left her first job as a salesclerk because she could not bear to watch when bananas were given to people with connections instead of being sold to the public. She left a training program in a school cafeteria because she refused to attend the mandatory course in "Marxist-Leninist political schooling," the "narrow, one-way road [that] didn't allow for discussion." She found unfair the practice of filling up choice vacation spots with Party members, while she was told that there was no room for a family of five.

The GDR *prided itself on its commitment to feeding and housing all its citizens, but Eva P. saw the difficulties women faced every day just to put food on the table. She felt that her "entire life had been a waste" because she had worked hard all her life, spent money on low quality merchandise, and now had nothing to show for it. By "nothing," she meant no things of quality. The Trabi cost her family East Marks 25,000, for example, but was not a good automobile. "I would like to buy everything all over again," she commented.*

Eva P. acknowledged the benefits provided by the state, for example, the services for women with children, but she never sent her children to day care, preferring to raise them within the family. She resented younger women who took advantage of

the child supports by staying home to take care of sick children, even when "it was only a sniffle." She added, "The older women had to work for the younger women." Given her history, it is not surprising that she was so optimistic about the Wende. *Contributing to that positive attitude was the fact that both she and her husband were employed, and, even though her children's jobs were in question, she was confident that the future would be bright. Greeting the* Wende *with enthusiasm and hope, she belongs to the large group of* GDR *citizens for whom the availability of fresh fruit and vegetables was an important aspect of individual liberty.*

Eva P.

When the old government collapsed, it was wonderful. It was a feeling that I can hardly describe. It had all started in 1945, and then when the Wall went up in 1961 we thought, that's it. It was like an open-air prison. Our generation felt it particularly strongly. The children, the third generation, grew up with it, so they never knew anything else. But my generation had been able to go anywhere we wanted and then suddenly we couldn't. For us the world had come to an end. So we saw the *Wende* as very positive. Now I don't feel locked in anymore; I feel truly free. We just took a trip to the Baltic Sea, and even though we didn't go any further, we knew if we had the money we could.

Now we have to do without some things because our salaries are still quite low. My husband is still getting his old salary of Marks 1200 a month. But we're very happy. At least we can buy fresh fruit and vegetables. Before we simply had to do without. In winter there were apples of various kinds, red cabbage and white cabbage, and green cabbage for Christmas. It was difficult for us women to shop and to cook. The greatest portion of our day was spent doing these activities, standing in lines, for example. If you went to the butcher you had to stand in line. If you wanted vegetables you had to stand in line. If you got to two stores that was a lot, and then you had to rush around to get your housework done. Now everything is much simpler. I have my money in my pocket, I buy what I want, and then I go home. Even if the stores are a little crowded it still goes quickly at the cash register. Before, we were told what we could buy, and that was all there was. For me personally it is a tremendous relief.

Women with small children, though, will have a hard time. They're already having a hard time. The former East German state supported women with children. At the same time this practice had very negative consequences. In factories and offices, when children got sick these young mothers stayed home. They had six weeks during which they received 90 percent of their salary and so they stayed home, even if it was only a sniffle. And this led to the setback in the economy because it was exploited too much. Now the young mothers have to pay the consequences. They have to work hard and can't take time off, and that will be difficult for them.

Women worked for a variety of reasons. Single women simply had to. What were they supposed to live on? In the case of married women, when we wanted to buy something big, such as a car or a colored television, that was a luxury. The average income was Marks 1000 per month, maybe 1200, including extra pay for night shift. In 1984 we bought a Japanese TV that cost over Marks 6000. At the end even the Trabi cost Marks 25,000, and we had to wait over twenty years for it. There was the Trabant and the Wartburg. The Trabi was robust but was loud and very bad for the environment.

I have three daughters, but none of them went to day care. My grandmother helped me with the housework, so I was able to work. At first I was trained as a saleswoman, but I left sales because black-market activities had gotten so bad that I couldn't stand it anymore. When there were bananas and not enough for everyone who wanted them, the people who got them were not our customers. Then there was trouble. The bananas weren't put out on the counter; it all happened under the table. There were lots of people who wanted bananas, and if we had sold them by the piece, lots of people could have bought five or six bananas. But no, the bananas were bought in crates in the back room. My conscience wouldn't allow me to work like that. That was before we moved to Berlin in 1980.

Here in Berlin I worked for ten years as a secretary for the Protestant church in the department for voluntary activities. I started but never completed the training program for a job in inventory at a school cafeteria. After the initial two years I was supposed to finish the program with a course in Marxist-Leninist political philosophy, but it was all politics which I rejected, so I refused to attend the course, and then I quit. It was just stupid political stuff. My daughters who all had to go through it told me they were happy that I never had to be submitted to it. They said it all just went in one ear and out the other, and they don't remember any of it today. They had to learn it in order to get through their program and then it was gone. It was all one-sided and monotonous. Our family was lower-middle-class and so we weren't able to go to college and, in order to make a decent living, we had to go through training programs which involved this political philosophy. The whole system was a narrow, one-way road and didn't allow for discussion. Even the smallest discussion was watched.

Three years ago I retired and was given an invalid's pension. Then I was allowed to work half-time for the church again, but the office work was too hard on my back and so I had to quit. I need lots of movement. My back wasn't operable, and so I grew vegetables at home. But at some point you have to be among people, and since I like to keep a nice home I decided to clean other people's homes.

If it hadn't been for the war I might have been able to fulfill my life's dream and become a nurse. But after the war in 1945 I got typhus. All of us got it. And after the war there wasn't enough medicine or not the right medicine and so I got very sick. I was taken to East Berlin's best hospital, the Charité, and given therapy. I wanted to be normal like other children, but I ended up with this hunch back. Otherwise I'm okay and my children were all born normal and so I'm very happy.

There were some good things here in East Germany that should be kept, such as many of the social programs for the elderly and for the handicapped. But as I said before, the programs for women were taken advantage of. I know a woman who had five children and was never married. She lived with a man, hardly ever went to work but still received her salary every month as well as her *Kindergeld*. The older women had to work for the younger women.

I worked hard and I spent lots of money. Now I have nothing of quality to show for it. Every person is a little bit egotistical when it comes to his or her personal life; everyone would like to have a little kingdom and be able to say, it was worth all the hard work and the personal cost. That wasn't the case with us. When we were young we worked our fingers to the bone from morning to night. I bought a knitting machine, and in the evenings I knitted for the children because knitted things were so expensive. Of course I spent a lot of money for it, and then it didn't work right. The sweaters were too small or too stiff, and then the kids wouldn't wear them.

We worked hard so that the family would have contact with some culture, some nice things, good manners. The kids didn't learn manners at school. They didn't learn that they should greet people on the stairway in the apartment house, even if it's three times on the same day. My daughters still do that. My daughters also say that everything—all the hard work—was all for nothing. Everything that we bought, whether it was a pair of shoes or a pair of socks, was money thrown out the window. No quality. Now if I have the time, I can look around and find things of quality for a small amount of money. I don't always have to go to an expensive store. I would like to buy everything all over again. I would like to be twenty again.

We took advantage of what was offered to us. For example, we went camping on the Baltic Sea. They never gave us a vacation spot because there wasn't enough room for five people, and although my husband and I could have requested a spot through the union, the FDGB, there was never enough room for the whole family. I didn't want to go if there wasn't enough room for my children. Vacation spots were only for SED Party members, for the big bosses, the *Bonzen*. They had everything: the biggest homes, the villas, all the things that we have just recently been able to see on TV. Before, we could only see these houses from the outside when we went for walks on the Baltic Sea.

My oldest daughter works in a home for disturbed children. She is single with one child. Right now it's hard for her, but I told her the sun will shine again for her soon. My second daughter is a nurse and has two children. The future of her job is also uncertain. The clinics are being closed, and the doctors don't know whether they'll be able to open a private practice or not. When her little boy is a little bigger she can go to West Berlin and find a job. They need nurses there and the pay is much better. If she gets a job in West Berlin she will have a four-week trial period, and even if she stays here she might have to have an additional training period. She hasn't worked for a couple of years and would have to learn how to work with all the new instruments.

My third daughter is single and is a psychiatric nurse. She received her training at the Charité Hospital and completed the program with very high marks. But she ran smack into politics. Every four weeks she was supposed to attend the Marxist-Leninist political philosophy course. She went two or three times and thought it was a waste of time and so she stood up and said her patients were more important to her and left. Of course they made life difficult for her. Six months later she applied for permission to leave the country, and four weeks after that they took out our telephone. So she moved over to West Berlin, and two months later they opened the border. None of us could find any meaning in the political stuff. All of us thought it was stupid. I remember when the girls came home from school. Whenever they threw their books down on the floor and carried on I knew what was the matter: they had had politics at school that day, *Staatsbürgerkunde*.

It will take awhile, but when the old is gone, I am very hopeful that things will be better. I'm very hopeful because we're all willing to work. There were lots of places where people didn't work hard or did sloppy work or didn't work at all. Then there were all the people in uniform, all the officers and soldiers who didn't do anything the whole day and were paid for it. That's what our tax money went for. It was too much. And then the secret police, the Stasi. We felt watched even when we went into a store. That's not an exaggeration. All our relatives had a Stasi file. We had one too. Life was hard and it was not pretty, but now it will be better. We have hope.

Everything is getting better. Now after a hard day I can afford to buy something nice for myself, even if it's only a chocolate bar. Before, that wasn't possible. Before, if I got a chocolate bar I saved it for my grandchildren. At Christmas there were oranges and we had to stand in line and could only buy them a few at a time. When Santa Claus came we had to be sure to get some. Berlin got preferential treatment because the entire government and the Stasi were in Berlin. In the rest of the country, it was really sad. In these last few years when I was at home I stood in line for oranges, even if it took days to finally get some, and if I could get only two kilos I took home two kilos. Then I gave some to my brother and his three children and my three children. We all took care of each other. Lots of people came to Berlin to shop because they couldn't get oranges anywhere else. You don't need to have an abundance of things, and I feel sick when I see the mountains of food in the department store Ka De We, but you need to be able to get certain items if you want them. It's so nice that those times are past. Now I can buy myself a small bag of nuts and they taste good, and they're worth the money, and that's it.

We're happy now. We go to bed satisfied and confident that no one will tell our children what to do. I'm responsible for my own life and can't depend on other people or on the state. I have ears and eyes so that I can work and live and get myself through. I'm thankful for every day that goes well. I enjoy sitting at home after work with my children and grandchildren. I feel good. We're free.

July 1992

Eva P. was not available for a second interview.

Helga Schütz,
fifty-five, writer and filmmaker

March 1991

I visited Helga Schütz on March 8—International Women's Day—in her house opposite the formerly state-owned DEFA *film studio in Potsdam-Babelsberg. In contrast to most of the women I interviewed, she lived not in an apartment, but in a two-story house with lovely hardwood floors, tasteful furniture, large rooms, and a huge parklike backyard. When I told her I wanted to ask her about the* Wende, *she laughed and said that she had already been asked to talk quite a lot about it. Indeed, an interview with Helga Schütz appeared in* Die Zeit *("Was 'n klein-kariertes Volk" ["What a small-minded people"] May 3, 1991), and a contribution of hers was published in a 1991 Luchterhand volume entitled* Gute Nacht, du Schöne [Good Night, You Beauty].

Helga Schütz smarted under the accusation of cowardice leveled against GDR *writers by the West German media after unification. Writers were not cowards, she said; they simply knew how far they could go in order to maintain the delicate balance between palatable criticism and criticism that would land them in jail. As she pointed out, writers found themselves in a dilemma whenever they read from a text they considered brave. Inspired by the reading, members of the audience might go home and stage a protest for which they were thrown in jail—while the writers themselves sat comfortably at home, protected by their publicity.*

Helga Schütz was ambivalent about the Wende. *On the one hand, she was relieved that now everyone could enjoy some of same privileges she had enjoyed, such as travel to the West. On the other hand, she was disappointed that the new German state had not become the ideal that she had envisioned. She had hoped that once the dream of an open border had come true, other political goals would be realized, such as the dissolution of the military.*

Helga Schütz lived for eighteen years in Großglienicke with the Wall in her backyard; now she was relieved to be out from under its shadow. "I never felt like a citizen of the German Democratic Republic; I felt a part of something bigger, maybe Europe."

Helga Schütz

Just before the *Wende* I was in Washington, D.C., and heard the news about the demonstrations on October 7 and 8. I was terribly afraid and of course also full of hope. I went right home. In September 1989, a group of writers had sent a letter to the Central Committee of the Party protesting the blatant misrepresentation by the GDR press of the mass emigrations of young people through the Hungarian border. We couldn't stand the lies any longer. Because of the serious confrontations in September, I had the feeling that things would be very tough in October.

When I got home in the middle of October, things had reached a climax. There were big Monday night demonstrations in Leipzig and also here in Potsdam in front of the Stasi jail and Stasi headquarters. Then there was a meeting of New Forum in the Friedrichskirche here in Babelsberg very near where I live. I attended that too. A group of women writers who had been meeting for years in Berlin went together to the November 4 demonstration at Alexanderplatz. Then things really began to happen.

It was clear to me that the Wall had to come down. I felt very strongly about that, even before the Hungarian border was opened. Whenever people spoke about *glasnost* and *perestroika* and demanded freedom to travel, I knew that it wouldn't be possible to open the Wall only a little bit, for only a few people to be allowed to travel, or for a certain number of people to be able to have a look at the other side. There would always be control on travel. But even so, November 9 was a tremendous surprise for me. I thought the announcement meant an easing of travel restrictions, but I expected that people would still have to apply for permission to travel and that only a small number would be granted that permission. I knew that our people would simply not be satisfied with that. The Wall had to go. But I imagined it would happen differently. I thought the Wall would disappear overnight, that they would come with hammers and wheelbarrows and take it away. It didn't happen like that of course, but the whole thing had a strong sense of the irrational to it. It was very hard to comprehend.

I lived for eighteen years with the Wall in my backyard in Großglienicke, on the border to West Berlin, and we talked about the Wall every single day of the year, how inane it was. You could hear people on the other side talking but you would have been shot if you had tried to talk to them. When the Wall was finally down, we rode our bikes over every evening with hammers and chopped away at it, trying to get it out of our sight. We would ride along the Wall, looking for a hole that was big enough to slip through. It was completely crazy. Suddenly you could walk where only weeks or days before you would have been shot.

On November 9 I came home at around midnight. I had been giving a reading in West Berlin. On the bus I heard some people saying that now everyone would be allowed to travel; they had heard it on the radio. When I got to my stop, there was a group of young people who said that they wanted to take the bus back to West Berlin. The driver told them to get on if they thought it would work. Then we saw the first Trabis driving in the direction of the border. When I got home my son and I sat and watched TV, intoxicated with joy. We watched the entire night. The next day he told me that they were going to open the Glienicke Bridge at 6:00 P.M., so we all marched over the bridge, the entire city of Potsdam. I was with friends of my son's, and we simply floated across the bridge. It was pure joy. We hadn't been able to take any champagne with us, but when we crossed over to the West they gave us some.

It was wonderful for me that it was no longer a privilege to cross the border— now everyone could cross. I had always had the feeling that our people here were being deceived; they didn't know what was really going on over there because they couldn't see it. There were great misconceptions. When I was in the West I felt I could do without many things that were available there: I didn't need that pair of shoes, that book. Then I got home and realized that I really did need those things. My son wanted a certain record, for example. They were little things, but because you couldn't get them they represented paradise. Now everyone could finally see this paradise themselves. They could touch it and realize that they could actually live without it. But they had to experience it first before they could start to reexamine their own values.

I wanted unification, but I wanted it to be different. Once this one dream of an open border had come true I thought all the other dreams could come true as well, for example, that we would get rid of the military. I never thought we would automatically have to join NATO. Just how great my illusions were has been demonstrated by the involvement of Germany in the Persian Gulf War. As soon as Germany's East-West conflict was solved, the Gulf War followed immediately.

I see unification as positive because I don't think there was any other way. That's the way the world is, and we have to accept it, even though there have been innumerable mistakes and huge catastrophes. Thousands of people are unemployed and yet there is so much work to be done just lying around on the streets. I wasn't a supporter of the so-called Third Way, the establishment of a democratic but separate East German state. I think Europe can only act reasonably if it's united. We all have to get past our own private sphere and come together. I didn't feel like a citizen of the German Democratic Republic; I felt a part of something bigger, maybe Europe. We Europeans had a common history and I never had the feeling that the common cultural heritage between West and East had been broken off. I knew that the Western economy functioned better than ours—not because it was a consumer society, a throw-away society—but because they paid much more attention to the environment than we did. The shortages didn't bother me as much as the fact that our economic system treated the environment so badly.

I'm very happy to be rid of all of the bureaucracy and the hassles that were part of our everyday existence. Whenever I got an invitation to a reading in the West I had to go to the Writers' Association (*Schriftstellerverband*), to make a travel application. After about six weeks I got a visa. If I had several invitations within a two- or three-week period I could get a visa that was good for more than one visit, which was wonderful because I knew that if I wanted to leave the country I could. I thought about leaving, but I never did it because of my children, and besides I'm a rather sedentary person. It was a beautiful feeling to know that the Wall was penetrable, but I couldn't see leaving the children behind this Wall forever and ever. They had a right to travel and see things. In the last three or four years I thought less and less about leaving.

When I applied for permission to go to Oberlin College to teach for a semester I was rejected twice before I was finally allowed to go. I still don't know why. I have my file from the Writers' Association—after the fall of the old regime we were sent our files—and there is a document about my application. The document includes a long conversation between me and the officials who tried to make me see that I was selling myself by going. Oberlin wanted to pay me a stipend for the three months of my stay—I couldn't live on air alone, and the East Mark was worthless in the United States—so I had signed a contract which stated that I would receive so many dollars a month. That was considered selling myself, illegal activity with foreign currency. Then I had to swear that I had been required to sign the contract in order to get a visa from U.S. immigration—they needed to know how I was going to live for those three months. I complained twice very openly to the appropriate officials here and finally they gave me the visa. Before you were issued a visa, your application went before twelve different institutions. All this was tremendously time-consuming and expensive.

Membership in the Writers' Association did not depend on Party membership. You only had to have published books. When I joined, there was an organization of young writers here in Potsdam, as there was in every district. We had readings once a month, and one writer sponsored me. I liked the Writers' Association, but I didn't like the fact that it became more and more involved with travel permits and that it developed into an extended arm of the Party. There were discussions about literature, but these became fewer and fewer. Primarily we dealt with cultural and political issues.

Of course I thought about leaving the Writers' Association, but where else would I have gone? Writers who weren't in the organization had to go to the Ministry of Culture to get their travel visas—you had to go to some institution or other. When I wanted to go to Großkochberg, a castle in Weimar where writers and other artists could stay inexpensively, I called the Writers' Association and they arranged it for me. Or I could stay at the old residence of Bettina von Arnim, another place where artists could live and work in peace and quiet. The Writers' Association also dealt with matters of health insurance and made sure people got their pensions. If you wanted something in this society you had to have an institution behind you, whether you wanted a new apartment or wanted to travel abroad. If you wanted to visit a factory, you needed a slip of paper with the proper signature and letter head. Nothing was possible for the individual private person, nothing at all. Without the Writers' Association I felt rather helpless.

I saw my role as a writer in this society as writers all over the world see their role in society, only increasingly I came to perceive that I wasn't writing for people outside the GDR but instead for those who lived inside this Wall, for my neighbors. This created considerable problems. I had to write about the many things that didn't appear in our media, and so I had to work more like a journalist. The subject matter ended up being very provincial. I could never concentrate simply on form; I was constantly interrupted by daily matters. Everyday life intruded into everything I wrote.

I tried to convince myself that I wasn't interested in being critical of our society, but I was. I wrote within the context of the literature that existed,

GDR literature. If one writer approached one forbidden subject in his writing, I would touch on another. We didn't discuss this among ourselves, but we knew what others were writing about. We read everything. Out of this context emerged my own writing. My writing always had the goal of expanding the limits of what was possible.

In the GDR there was censorship. You knew where the allergic spots were, what points were supposed to be avoided; you simply knew. You felt you had a duty to mention one of these allergic points. Not that you necessarily wanted to make Honecker angry; it was nothing quite so primitive or direct. It was indirect. I don't know if literature can actually change anything. Its task is more to create a sense of solidarity among people. Readers who feel that they are only a tiny fraction can get a sense of the whole; they can find themselves in the piece of literature they are reading.

But I didn't write with readers in mind. I wrote for myself. But I wrote also for the people who know me and for the people who don't know me. I wrote for my neighbors but also for people who had no idea what I was trying to do, somewhere in between. But I also wrote for my own pleasure. It would be terrifying if I realized that I was trying to write to please someone else, a literary critic or public opinion. You can't escape from these people, but you don't have to write intentionally for them. I enjoyed writing, even when it was hard. I wanted to form language. Language always has many meanings, and this variety of meanings attracted and fascinated me. It's not that I want to explain certain things; some things always remain a secret to me too. Today I read my early books a little differently than I did when I wrote them. If that weren't so, I wouldn't have to bother; my work would be lifeless.

With regard to GDR literature, I would say that the books that appeared in the last four years dealt increasingly with the everyday lives of the people; they are stamped with the daily life here. For that reason they don't have the glow of the earlier books; they're not as elastic. I'm not so sure I would want to read them again years later. There's only one word to describe them: provincial. Literature perhaps was able to effect change, because the people who bought them—and the books always had large print runs—were in a sense performing a political act. There was a great desire to own a book, to go to readings; people wanted to identify more with the writers than the politicians. Huge numbers of people who didn't really have any great knowledge of or interest in literature as such bought these books and were brought together because of the notion of resistance that the books contained. The state always referred to the GDR as a "nation of readers," which was true, but there was a certain amount of conspiracy in this reading.

West Germans are criticizing East German writers now for having been cowards, but the little bit that we did was all that you could manage; it was all you could get away with. You couldn't throw too many things into the balance because that would have destroyed the equilibrium. Everyone was interested in coexistence. No one dared to confront the largest, most important problems, not writers, not anyone. Writers weren't cowards; they just knew how far they could go. If I held a reading of a text that I considered terribly brave in which I talked about refusing military service, for example, and I had a forum of young people who hung on every word and thought I was a terrific role model, these young people then went home and said, "Let's stage a protest at school." They got thrown in jail while I sat comfortably at home. This was a terrible conflict for me. I tried to avoid reading texts like that. I was always aware that nothing would happen to me because I was protected by my notoriety.

I was aware of the privilege I enjoyed and made it one of the themes in my last books. I had to. I couldn't talk about anything that happened outside the Wall without bringing up the topic of privilege. It was always one of the main conflicts. Maybe I was trying to come to terms with it myself by writing about it. I wondered why people who were fairly well known didn't fight for the same privilege I had. For example, I couldn't understand why academics didn't refuse to work if they weren't allowed to travel to a certain conference. But this is an example of the not very well thought-out reproaches we leveled against one another. The fact that I was an artist with no boss to answer to was one of the privileges I enjoyed.

The people in the West who criticized us the loudest were the ones who wanted to keep everything intact here. For example, I made a film for a West German TV station about the city of Rostock. At the risk of my life—no, not that great—but at great risk, I tried to show the disintegration that was occurring in Rostock. Someone was always watching me during the filming, but when he left for a few minutes I told the cameraman to take a certain house which was falling apart or other evidence of the actual condition of the city—not only the lovely facade but the real interior—to show what our cities really looked like. I tried to get these things into the film, even though I knew that I would have great problems when I got home and people saw it on TV.

But censorship also occurred in the West. The editors of this particular TV station thought the film was unkind and cold; they wanted to see only the beautiful GDR. That was very sweet of them, but it wasn't the whole truth, and if you tried to show a piece of the truth they wouldn't play along. They didn't want to see the true picture. For this same reason they received Honecker with great pomp and ceremony. It was all done in the name of compromise. And now it's the writers alone who are said to have been the cowards. The people in the West wanted to believe that everything here was all right, and now they're shocked and surprised at how things really were. Maybe they should have read our books more carefully and watched our films more attentively, and maybe they should have looked more closely when they took their trips through the GDR.

I had two children: a daughter, who was severely disabled and died when she was twelve, and a son. I was never married, but filmmaker Egon Gunther and I lived together for a long, long time. The issue of "illegitimate children" here in the GDR was completely unimportant. No one cared about who would inherit what and what money belonged to whom because the money wasn't worth anything. There was something to be said for living in a society where money didn't play a big role. I always had my daughter with me, and I think I started writing because I wanted to do something I could do at home. My daughter actually brought me to writing. I can't complain, although it was difficult, because I felt so enriched through Claudia.

Women here were emancipated, but it was tremendously difficult for them because they had to fight for their everyday existence. But they managed to come away with their piece of the pie. All around me here are women who worked because they wanted to and wouldn't have given that up. In comparison to women in West Germany and the United States, women here look very gray. Our women look worn out and don't fit the image of Western women. You can't see their emancipation on the outside. But you can see on the inside that they have worked, that they are independent, and that they know life. They also experienced the solidarity that this difficult daily existence brought with it. I don't know if this sort of thing exists in the West; I don't know the West well enough. But I must say, I was very impressed with the solidarity I saw in U.S. women. In 1984 I went to the Women in German (WiG) meeting in Boston with very mixed feelings. I thought, oh dear, I'm going to be in a group of women who feel they have gotten the short end of the stick in a man's world and are trying to assert themselves any way they can. I was very pleasantly surprised that it wasn't like that at all, and I was a little envious. Such conscious opposition wouldn't have been possible here. Here things happened under the surface.

July 1992

The time between the two interviews was a productive one for Helga Schütz, in terms of both her writing and her filmmaking. She was invited by the West German city of Mainz to spend a year there as writer in residence (Stadtschreiberin). *Wanting to escape the preoccupation with the* Wende *that she experienced all around her, she traveled to the former Soviet Republic of Kazakhstan at the end of that year to gather material for a film that was shown on ARD television. This trip also produced the book* Heimat süße Heimat. [Homeland, Sweet Homeland], *published by Aufbau. At the time of this writing she was working on the screenplay for a feature film about a jailed Kazakhstan actor as well as preparing two documentary films. One of these will look at educational reform in the early days of the* GDR; *the other will examine the child-rearing formulas from the 1950s in the* GDR *and the sense of guilt* (Schuld) *between parents and children resulting from these practices.*

After recounting her many professional activities, she mentioned that she was startled every time she heard Wessi *friends talk about going for a walk or a bike ride along the* Todesstreifen, *the wide, desolate "death strip" where the Wall once stood. Still conscious of the shadow it cast for twenty-eight years, she thought it would be a long time before the memory of the Wall had receded far enough for East Germans to be able to do the same.*

Heike Prochazka,

twenty-nine, lifeguard and
water-safety instructor

February 1991

Heike Prochazka worked as a lifeguard in a public pool in Berlin. She was paid, as she said, quite well—DM 1000 per month. She was resentful, however, that a lifeguard she knew in the western half of the city earned DM 2800 for doing the same thing. At least Heike Prochazka's job was not being eliminated, as many were: her pool in the district of Friedrichshain had been taken over by the new Berlin government. Still she would be required to complete a training program designed to certify her according to West German standards. In addition, she would have to fill out the "infamous questionnaires regarding the political past." Her activity as a Party functionary (APO Sekretär) would be scrutinized and might jeopardize her chances of keeping her job.

Heike Prochazka loved the GDR, identified strongly with it, and was proud of it. Born in 1961, she belonged to the generation that grew up with the Wall as a constant presence, and although border crossings were located only several hundred meters from her apartment, she said that she did not feel locked in. She was able to come to terms with the Wall by seeing it within the context of the country she loved: "I never pretended it was something it wasn't." This attitude was in part a result of having been a member of an elite group: as a young girl she was groomed to become an Olympic swimmer. Furthermore, she absorbed the positive relationship to the GDR professed by her mother, who had joined the Party just after the new state was formed in 1949. Heike Prochazka was angry that she had to exchange her Heimat for a new country she did not choose.

Perhaps this anger prompted the ambivalence in her comments. She disliked the system which required people like her brother to join the Party to get ahead professionally, but she was more critical of her brother and the people who ac-

quiesced to the system than she was of the Party. She was grateful that she had been able to "live [her] homosexuality" in the GDR, *while at the same time she acknowledged that the attitudes toward lesbians were not as hostile as they were toward male homosexuals. Although she never had any negative experiences with the state because of her homosexuality, she did experience pain in her personal life because of societal attitudes.*

Heike Prochazka was greatly affected by the Wende. *As a result, she had ceased her former political activity, although she promised engagement again in the future. She spoke for many who were pleased with the niche they had found in the* GDR *and were being forced to start over.*

Heike Prochazka

My mother raised four kids alone. When we were about nine or ten my twin sister and I started swimming competitively. I liked the feeling of togetherness in the group, the common goal of high achievement, and the recognition that it brought to the GDR. We were prepared psychologically and politically so that if we swam against another country we knew we represented the GDR. I attended the sports school for three years here in Hohenschönhausen. It's closed now, and only a few of the old sports schools will continue. We had practice three times every day and a full training program—plus our regular classes—all at the same school. In the seventh grade I was put into a so-called concentration group, which consisted of the best athletes who received a more intensive training. My mother had to give her permission for this, because it meant I would be going to school for thirteen years but would only finish with a tenth-grade education instead of a high school diploma because we would spend more time swimming and less time in classes. I was in this concentration group for two months and then was forced to quit because I slipped a disk. I was thirteen.

I really enjoyed the swimming, although I have to say that there were things that I wasn't able to do as a child because I spent all my time swimming. But I wanted to. I don't feel as though I missed anything. My sister had to quit around the same time I did because she wasn't developed enough to be a strong swimmer. I told the trainer to wait a bit because I knew she would grow, and she did. But then it was too late.

For swimmers at that age there were meets only in other socialist countries. We were very good, and our performance was very important for the GDR.

Partly through these sports events—and the swimmers made a major contribution to this—the GDR was recognized outside the socialist bloc. It was a big problem that the GDR wasn't recognized by the rest of the world. That was one reason that sports were promoted so strongly. We were given everything we needed. Every year we got new equipment: warm-up suits, bathing suits, tennis shoes—everything that we needed to perform well—for only Marks 5. And fantastic meals. There was also a boarding school there for people who lived outside Berlin, and they only had to pay Marks 10 a month. When I was swimming no one took drugs. We didn't take any pills or shots, only vitamin pills. Some people think that these sports programs were overvalued and promoted too heavily by the state. But of course people who were actually involved had a very different point of view. For example, people blamed the swimming program for the fact that I hurt my back so seriously, but I could have hurt it doing something else just as easily. That's my attitude.

When I was fourteen, I became a swimming instructor at a training center. These kids were being groomed for one of the sports schools. After ten years at this job, it became clear to me that I didn't get along very well with children. Also there was the additional problem that I had to convince the parents to send their kids to sports school and I felt pretty guilty doing it. They came to me and said, "We've heard that the program is hard on the kids' health," and I was supposed to convince them that it was okay, and there I was with an injured back myself. That contradiction was too much for me, so I quit.

I had always wanted to be a swim coach at one of the sports schools, but because of my back they wouldn't accept me into the training program. I had to do something, so I went into a two-year apprenticeship program for customer service. This profession doesn't exist any more. It will probably be restructured in the way it is in West Germany. The job meant dealing with customers. For example, if you came to me with a broken vacuum cleaner, four weeks later you could pick it up and I was responsible for everything that happened in those four weeks. I had to write out the appropriate forms for sending it out, then the delivery people came and took it to the repair shop, and then returned it repaired.

But I still wanted to be a swim coach. So in 1979 I completed a lifesaving program, which also doesn't exist here any more. It was a three-month program and at the end I had a second area I could work in. I got a job as a lifeguard, but somehow I didn't feel satisfied. I sat on the edge of the pool at age twenty-two and thought, is this all there is? And so I decided I wanted to go to college. I didn't know what I wanted to study, but I knew I had to get out of the swimming pool.

I finally decided to study GDR public administration. This doesn't exist anymore either because the GDR doesn't exist. I started the program in Weimar in 1988. All of us in this program had already had practical experience in administration, and when the instructors talked theory to us, we frankly told them that that wasn't the way things worked in the real world, but the instructors insisted on hammering their theories into us. That was a terrible contradiction. I knew people who had completed the three-year program and when they went back to their districts to work, full of energy and new ideas, they couldn't get anywhere with their department heads. So many simply left.

Then came the *Wende*. It was a blow for me. When the border was opened on November 9, I couldn't comprehend it. I was still in Weimar. The border opened on a Thursday, and we took the train to Berlin on the weekend. The train was packed, and the champagne corks were flying, but I didn't feel optimistic. Not because I knew what was coming, but because I was born in 1961—the year the Wall was built—and had grown up in this country. I was raised by a very progressive mother who had been one of the first to join the Party in 1949. In addition, because of the competitive swimming, I had a very positive relationship with the GDR. I had been able to do everything I wanted. I had never had any problems with the state because of my homosexuality. The Wall ran right along here, but I never had the feeling that I was locked in or a prisoner, as some are saying now. I'm a different generation. I grew up with it. I was always able to defend it with a clear conscience, and I never pretended to myself that it was something that it wasn't. Then suddenly the Wall was open.

It took a long time for me to get up the nerve to go across the border. It was very strange. Then I could only stand it there for a half hour. Still now I feel so happy when I'm back in my own four walls, my familiar environment. Yesterday we were "over there," or as you're supposed to say now, in the western part of the city. You can see how hard it is for me to get used to this new terminology. I grew up with it all, and I can't just take it off like an old coat the way so many people are doing. They turned in their Party books and joined the CDU. Absolutely sick. I wonder what kind of Party members they were anyway. It's because of people like these that the Party went to pieces.

In this drastically changed situation, I had to decide whether to continue my studies, studies that would have led to my being a civil servant (*Beamtin*). I decided I don't want to be a civil servant because I have no intention of being a part of this new system which I didn't want. You would have to leave who you were on the coat rack with your coat, go to work and say yes and amen to everything, do your work well—that's a normal expectation—then you would come home at night and put your person back on and then you could do what you wanted. But I wasn't raised that way. I always expressed my opinion at work if I didn't like something, and that had nothing to do with fact that I was in the Party. I would have done it anyway. As a civil servant you can't express your opinion, and you can't be political at all, and I was always very political.

There were some terrible things going on at the college where I was studying in Weimar. Many of the instructors there, who had taught socialist law with great conviction for twenty or thirty years, were now suddenly teaching capitalist law with equal conviction and were saying that that was what they'd wanted all the time. I ask you, how could anyone stand that? During the exams in the summer of 1990, well after the *Wende,* I heard that they were still testing students in the various fields of law, family law, criminal law, administrative law, according to socialist criteria. They were still teaching that in the summer of 1990. How schizophrenic! I left the program on May 30, 1990, and started working here at the pool again. It was the only thing I could do. I gave them my reasons in writing. I told them that what they were teaching had nothing to do with the reality outside, and that when I was finished in 1991 I wouldn't be able to understand anything that was happening around me.

I didn't leave the Party. The SED dissolved itself and renamed itself, or restructured itself into the PDS. One day it was called the SED, the next the PDS. We were given the opportunity to simply move over into the PDS by exchanging our old documents for new ones. But that didn't sit well with me, so I didn't. The PDS has very different goals because the conditions that exist now are very different. I don't think it should be called the successor party to the SED. Sure, there are many of the same people in it, but they have to think about things a bit, they have to change too. No one is saying that people in the old CDU here in the GDR are the same as the people in the new CDU, no one is saying, the "former East CDU" or "successor Party," even though it's the same people.

There were lots of things that the Party did which I didn't like. And I didn't like it that there were so many people in the Party for reasons of convenience or career, and there were unfortunately many, many, many. I can give an example from my own family. One of my brothers joined the Party only because he wanted to run a restaurant, not a private restaurant, but a Party-owned HO,

Handelsorganisation. The Party secretary in charge of restaurants told him that he had to join the Party, and since he wanted it, and because it's a very nice restaurant, he joined the Party. This sort of thing over forty years is very destructive.

Sometimes I have the feeling that I can't put my ideals into practice. On the contrary, they hold me back. Lots of people call me naive and say, "Your ideals aren't helping you at all. Look at us, look at what we've been able to accomplish!" So now I'm not politically active at all. On the one hand I can't identify with the new system, I don't want it, but I have no other choice. On the other hand I see that nothing can be done to change the situation. What difference does it make if I march through the streets or get involved? I'll have yelled myself hoarse and used up my energy, and the next day the newspaper will report the opposite of what happened. For me there is no point to getting involved with the political left because money decides everything. It's important to have an opposition, but I can't be a part of it right now. At some point I'll certainly get involved with women's issues and lesbian issues, but that's it.

In terms of my personal life, when I was in the tenth grade I noticed that I was very attracted to women. But I didn't even think about homosexuality. For me at that time relationships meant man, woman, and child. However, it did strike me that all my girlfriends had a boyfriend, and I wasn't interested. Of course I thought about this, but there was no one I could discuss it with. It wasn't talked about. I knew the term "feminist" and had heard of the women's movement, so I knew about independent women and thought I was probably one of those.

Then when I was seventeen I worked as a camp counselor and fell deeply in love with a woman named Hannelore. We didn't sleep together because we decided to wait until I was eighteen. It wasn't for legal reasons, since the laws on homosexuality never applied to women, only to men. And in 1972 the law restricting homosexual behavior, Paragraph 175, was taken out of the criminal code, so that wasn't an issue. We decided to wait because Hannelore was afraid of losing her teaching job. Up until that point I had been very introverted and didn't talk a lot. When I met Hannelore, overnight I was a changed person. I still had never heard of homosexuality, but I had seen two women living together, and I had seen my gay brother and his friend together. It was all very natural, and so I thought, okay, you're like that too. I had no problem with it. In fact, I was happy to have an answer to all the questions that kept turning around in my head: why I didn't have a boyfriend, why I wasn't interested in men. When I came home after two weeks at camp, my mother had a totally different daughter.

So she sent me to a psychologist. Even though she already had a gay son and lots of contact with gay men through her work in gastronomy, she couldn't handle the homosexuality of her daughter. Then she went to the school where Hannelore taught and talked to the principal. She said to her, "Your colleague seduced my daughter." She had decided Hannelore wasn't fit to be a teacher. How could a lesbian educate children? The principal liked Hannelore and respected her as a teacher, and she said to my mother, "So?" Hannelore was able to continue teaching at that school and is still there to this day. There were lots of gay men teachers who lived with this fear of being exposed on a daily basis. Things are a bit more open now so that gay men can teach without fear of losing their jobs, but in the past, in the GDR gay men simply weren't teachers.

I never had any negative experiences with the state because of my homosexuality. I always had good jobs, perhaps because it doesn't occur to anyone that I'm a lesbian. I know how to flirt with men. But if someone asked me what was going on with me—no one ever asked outright whether I was homosexual—it was always people who I knew very well and had a good relationship with, and it was something I wanted to talk about with them because that sort of openness is important in a good relationship. Their reaction was always very positive. They said, "Great, we have someone we can talk to about this." They had never had anyone they could talk to about it so they had a false image of homosexual relationships.

The role of the state in all this varied. My experience was that as long as you didn't give the Stasi any reason to go after you, they left you alone. The apartment I lived in for six years with my partner Monika was opposite the West German Permanent Mission—since the FRG didn't recognize the GDR it wasn't called a consulate—and twenty-four hours a day Stasi were stationed out in front. Stasi people most certainly lived in this house and knew everything that was going on here, and we were most certainly registered with the state security. But we never had any problems with the Stasi. Monika was afraid of being found out because she belonged to the *Reisekader,* the Party members who traveled, and the security surrounding these people was always very strict. Of course they had checked her personal life, and still she was allowed to travel. Nothing negative ever happened. But that was probably because we lived together for six years monogamously. If we each had had other relationships, that would have been different. In addition we were both in the Party and we both worked hard, so there was no reason to go after us.

There were definitely people who did have negative experiences, and they're the majority. My gay brother ran a cafe for four years before he bought it, and I know for a fact that the secret police were there. I assume that a file was created on every person who frequented the place. There were also gay men who had been pressured to work for the secret police. Any homosexual, whether man or woman, could be blackmailed by the Stasi: "If you don't work for us, we'll think of something. You'll lose your job and won't know why at first, but then you'll know it was us." So these people didn't have any choice. I talked about all this with the Stasi men at the cafe. People won't become tolerant if we don't come out of our closets. That's why I want to get involved in lesbian politics.

Many of the problems for women that have come with the *Wende* don't affect me: women and abortion, women and work. So I don't feel that I'm necessarily worse off now than I was before the *Wende*. I feel worse inside, but that's my personal inner perception. I don't think anything has changed with regard to society's attitude toward homosexuality because the people here in East Berlin haven't changed. But as far as the new society is concerned, gay people living in the East now have richer lives because they can go to West Germany, to the cafes, bars, discos. There's even a travel agency for homosexuals. These things are acknowledged and supported by the West German society. I'm bothered by a contradiction in West German society, though. On the one hand, homosexuality is recognized and accepted, but, on the other hand, the society sets certain limits. In the GDR I was able to live my homosexuality. Now I don't know how things will be.

July 1992

Heike Prochazka's adjustment to the new society was not as difficult as she had anticipated. Not only did she keep her job at the public pool, she had also started swimming competitively again. She said that she was now swimming for herself, not for the GDR—although she had been proud to swim for her country. "It's not political anymore. I'm fulfilling a childhood dream," she beamed. Swimming also provided an outlet for her frustrations. While others sat around and blamed external causes, she swam one thousand meters and regained her internal balance. She was amazed when her mother asked her whether she was being paid to swim and concluded that the question reflected the shift in values since the Wende. She thought that this materialism had perhaps been latent in many people in the GDR. "Maybe that's why so many people voted CDU," she laughed.

She worried that the opening of the Stasi files could compound feelings of guilt and mistrust among friends. Those who had worked for the Stasi might try to avoid people they had spied on, while those who had no Stasi connections might find out which of their friends had reported on them. She thought that the friendships she had now, though fewer, were more honest than they had been in the past.

When asked what had changed for her since our last interview, she said she was surprised at the more accepting attitude toward homosexuality. Although she had been afraid that she would not be able to live her homosexuality in the new Germany the way she had in the GDR, she said that she could be more open now than she had ever thought would be possible. In a buoyant mood, she joked that in general things weren't as different as she thought they would be: "There are still empty shelves and long lines."

Maria Curter,

forty-five, biologist, formerly at the
Academy of Sciences, now in an
environmental training program

January 1991

*When I arrived at the apartment of Maria Curter, I found her working over a stack
of insurance papers. Selecting the right insurance policy was for many one of the
most onerous tasks to be faced after unification. For Maria Curter, it symbolized
the unwelcome shift from the centralized socialist system of the GDR to the capitalist bureaucracy of the FRG. She saw much that had been good in the GDR. Among
other things, she appreciated the fact that many aspects of her life had been stable
and dependable. There was one centralized system for banking and insurance,
rents and prices for certain foods remained constant, and, as she observed, "You
could plan your life for years in advance." With the uncertainties brought by the
new bureaucracy following unification, this ability to plan so concretely for the
future had changed. However, she recognized that the state had exacted a toll for
its services. It had assumed the right to tell its citizens what to do, a right which she
said had intruded into her professional life: her university studies in environmental research were brought to a halt when the state was no longer interested in
environmental protection.*

*Maria Curter was one of several women interviewed who had chosen to have a
child without being married because of the generous supports provided by the state
for single mothers. She maintained, "For us a child was a child, and it didn't
matter whether the child was born to a single woman or a married one." However,
she admitted that she was sometimes viewed as a bad mother when she took full
advantage of the children's facilities and left her infant daughter, Peggy, at day care
for several days when she was out of town on business. The fact that Peggy's father
was a black African was not without consequences. As Maria Curter said, although*

the state encouraged single women to combine family and work, it made no attempt to address the issue of race in GDR society.

Maria Curter came to the GDR when she was eleven. In 1957 her mother had returned from Vienna to her native Berlin after losing her job as a physicist with a Russian firm. When Austria became neutral in 1955, she was unable to find another job. Maria Curter had lost her mother when she was sixteen and had made her own way in the GDR. The same feisty spirit that got her through a difficult youth was apparent at forty-five. Despite a pronounced anger at the process of unification, she said the Wende was very good because of the possibilities it brought. At the time of the interview she was taking advantage of the new opportunities to enroll in a training program in West German environmental law in order to become an environmental consultant.

Maria Curter

I studied biology and chemistry and taught school for a few years, and then I worked for fourteen years as an editor for a popular science magazine for young people. I went back to school for four years for a doctorate in environmental research, but I never finished my degree. All research on the environment was suddenly stopped for political reasons. They weren't interested in environmental protection any longer. At the beginning of the seventies we had very good environmental laws, and at international conferences I heard over and over how progressive our policies were. But by the end of the seventies whatever progress we had made had stopped, and at the beginning of the eighties all data regarding the environment became top secret, absolutely top secret.

This sort of thing happened fairly often. When a new political directive came out, certain research projects were suddenly broken off. No one was interested anymore, just as they were no longer interested in my work. For example, the Central Committee of the Party decided from one day to the next to shift the entire economy to brown coal. The minister for the environment wasn't even asked.

My old job was moved out of Berlin, so in 1983 I went to work at the Center for Scientific Information at the Academy of Sciences and began building an information system for environmental research. My project was approved, but no one was really interested in that either—they just needed an extra staff person. My job disappeared when the Wall opened. The entire Academy of Sciences has been dissolved. So I'm now in a retraining program to learn to become an environmental consultant. With this training I could get a job in industry, whether in East or West, I don't care.

The state took a lot off your shoulders, but it demanded something in return: the right to tell you what to do. They told us where and when we could travel, how we could invest our money—to the extent that any of us had any money to invest—and told us what we could buy. Having the state take over many things in your life meant you had to accept the other things that came along with it.

Now the citizens of the GDR have chosen the CDU and along with it certain inconveniences: now they have to take care of their own taxes and insurance policies. They no longer have a secure job, they no longer have inexpensive day care, and they can't plan for the next five years. But they have the freedom to travel and to the extent they have any money, they can invest it as they choose. I don't know what this all means. For me personally it's nothing but negative. I've lost my job, and I don't know what lies ahead.

The ideal social system has yet to be found: each one we've come up with so far has advantages and disadvantages. I was familiar with the advantages and disadvantages in the GDR. I could have left if the conditions here had been intolerable. I could have married outside the GDR, for example. There were always ways to get out. But I chose to stay. I was in the Party and was even asked to attend a school for Party functionaries, but I declined. I didn't want to get involved to that extent.

The socialist ideology always espoused equality for women in all areas of their development. When I was eighteen or nineteen I took this notion very seriously, and it was valid to a certain extent. Women could go to college if they wanted and were encouraged to go into typically male jobs, like construction. Women in fact went into engineering in large numbers. Women could work on equal footing with men and felt they could contribute equally, up to a certain point, that is. When women wanted to be more than just basic workers, things got more complicated. Then we heard such things as, "Yes, but your child gets sick so often."

Then in 1972 came the so-called social-political program, which I supported at the time although today I would see it more critically. Young marriages were encouraged, as were women with children. The idea was good: it ensured future generations. Young married couples received Marks 5000 which they had to pay back within five years, but without interest, quite a lot for us. The average monthly salary back then was about Marks 700 per month. This gave the young couple the chance to buy a washing machine and a refrigerator or furniture for an apartment. Women also received Marks 1000 for every child they bore. Then the state paid the family Marks 20 a month for the first child and more for each subsequent child. Families with lots of children also got benefits. A single mother with three children was considered "children rich," and her kids would have free meals at school; once a month she could use the laundry less expensively. Lots of young people took advantage of these benefits. At the same time women were given the opportunity to determine for themselves when they would have a child. The pill was introduced, and abortion became available to every woman during the first trimester. These social-political measures had their advantages and disadvantages. The advantages were that a woman could afford to take care of her child for the first two or three years—the first year after the birth she could stay home and receive 70 percent of her salary. But the negative side of it was that some women just stayed home and had children. The state couldn't afford that, especially if the state had paid for the woman's college education.

I was always very independent. I knew what I was capable of, and I never had to depend on anyone. That's how things were here. Women were economically independent. They never had the economic pressure to get married, and it was easy to get divorced. Men had no responsibilities after the divorce except to support their children. They didn't have to pay alimony. After the divorce men paid a certain percentage of their salary for child support, and that was the end of it.

The other side of the coin was that men took advantage of women's independence. They said, "If she's so independent, let her carry the coal up from the basement." A lot of the nice things that had to do with men's and women's roles disappeared. Women didn't get bouquets of flowers. Although lots of policies for women were very progressive, many of the attitudes remained traditional and middle class: women should really stay at home. No one admitted how widespread this attitude was.

By the time I was sixteen, both my parents were dead, and I had a younger brother to take care of. We were too old for an orphanage, and since no one was watching out for me I had to take care of myself. I wanted a husband and a family, but I didn't want a husband just so that I could say that I had a husband who earned well. I wanted a real partner, and since I hadn't found one by the time I was twenty-five, and since my biological clock was ticking, I decided to have Peggy then. I could always continue to look for a partner. The fact that I had a child without being married was simply not an issue. I only really became aware of a difference recently when I had to fill out my income tax forms. For us, a child was a child, and it didn't matter whether the child was born to a single woman or a married one. It was only important when it came to inheritance matters. All educational opportunities were the same. As a single mother, I never felt any discrimination.

However after the *Wende,* I was one of the first to be fired from my job at the Academy, I think because I was a single woman with a child. Two other women with the same degree that I have, whose husbands earn a good salary and who have no children, were not fired, nor were two women who threatened to go to court. I am suing them to rehire me. As long as I am in my retraining program, I will continue to get my salary. So if I don't get my job back, I'll at least get a salary. I don't want to harp on this business of single women with children, but it's true that men do try to get women like me—self-confident, competent women—out of the way. Maybe it's a kind of complex. They expect single women to come flying to them, and when that doesn't happen, they have to show that they're a man. It's macho. Of course, it depends on the individual people, on what kind of work you're talking about, what level of society. I wouldn't want to generalize about it.

My daughter's father was an African. I wanted to have a child, but the relationship didn't work out. I knew I could support one child, and I already had an apartment. One thing I didn't reckon with was that it made a difference to our men whether I had a child with an African or with a German. I've tested this. As long as we were just talking about my daughter, everything was okay. But as soon as I showed them a picture of her, they became very negative. "No, that's too much," they said. I think it has to do with men's psyche; I'm not sure that it necessarily has to do with racism. Of course there was prejudice, stronger prejudice than I would have thought, especially in certain segments of the population. You can't say everyone was prejudiced. It depended on people's experience with foreigners. At the beginning the only foreigners in the GDR were students. Later the foreign workers came, the Vietnamese, the Cubans, the people from Mozambique. Some folks said they were good workers; others said they were lazy whoring drunks. People didn't differentiate. The state brought only the men, not their families or their wives, so a lot of them had relationships with German women. It was hard for lots of people to accept that.

I wasn't discriminated against myself, but people did look at me. Whether I wanted to be or not, I was always the center of people's curiosity. My daughter, Peggy, wasn't discriminated against at school, but when she came into a new circle there was always this curiosity. She was exotic. Sometimes people called her "nigger." In cases like that the teachers would get involved. But her classmates didn't have a problem with the black-white issue, and my daughter was able to integrate fully into life at school. Out of three hundred children at her school, there were always two or three children of color. There was a boy from India, for example. But in comparison with Austria or Belgium there were not very many children of mixed race.

There was one problem that came up for my daughter, not so much because she was the child of an African, but because she was the child of a foreigner. She was very athletic, very good in track and field and she wanted to go to a sports school, but she wasn't accepted. Of course she wouldn't have been accepted either if her father had gone over to West Germany. It didn't have to do with race. It was that because she had relatives in the West there was a possibility that she might leave the GDR.

There was always prejudice, but there were never open, direct attacks. The prejudice was kept under wraps and came out as a kind of holding back, a kind of reserve. The Skinhead movement is definitely racist in its orientation, but that didn't originate here. It came over to us from West Germany. What was latent in our society is now being stirred up. The Skinheads have taken up the old Nazi ideology of Germanness and found a fertile ground for their ideas. Officially no one would have dared to express such ideas, even if they had wanted to. But there wasn't any reason to because there were no social conflicts of this kind. They were always smoothed over. Now that the Wall is down these social conflicts are surfacing, and people are hunting for the cause of the conflicts, confusing the cause with the effects. It's easy to put the blame on a minority, whether it's a racial minority or an economic minority. There was very little opportunity to let out aggression in the GDR, and the strict regime kept it that way. Now there are opportunities, which are also being provoked and artificially stirred up through the media.

I sent Peggy to *Kinderkrippe* and of course she went to day care. Some people thought I was a bad mother because I didn't keep her at home when she was tiny, but I was traveling a lot then, about ten days a month, not ten consecutive days, but two days here, three days there. Peggy was able to spend the night at day care and that saved me from having to go begging to friends for a favor of a night or two. She didn't have the advantage of two parents, but if I had it to do over again, I would do it exactly the same way.

Even though almost all women worked outside the home, services weren't set up to help them. There were no precooked meat dishes, for example, which you just had to heat up at home. When I finished work at 5:45 there was no time to take clothes to the laundry. It could have been centrally regulated with working women in mind. Another example which I noticed as a single woman: whenever I had to go to a government agency to take care of some small matter, the offices all closed at 6:00, and you had to get special permission from your boss to leave work early. On the other hand we had the so-called household day, the paid day of leave to take care of things like this, but if you had more than one thing to take care of, you couldn't do it in a day. And then the household day was only given to married women or women with children or women older than forty. Men didn't have it unless they had to take care of a child, but the people at work didn't much like it. They said to him, "Get yourself a girlfriend; she'll get a household day."

The *Wende* has been very good. I can now make my own decisions about where to live or what job to take. If I weren't so angry about how the unification has come about I could rejoice about all the possibilities. But I didn't choose the Federal Republic; I didn't voluntarily give up my job. These things were determined for me by others, and that makes me mad. I like to make my own decisions.

July 1992

Maria Curter found a job that was creative and satisfying. She—along with two hundred other unemployed academics—had secured a two-year ABM position to uncover neglected East Berlin history. Because ABM positions are temporary, she was actively seeking a permanent job in her field. In addition to writing for honoraria, she had traveled to a number of professional conferences in France, Belgium, England, Austria, and West Germany. In Austria she was able to return to the house where she was born.

Reflecting on the time since our first interview, she commented, "I'm still not happy with the way things are going." For example, her rent was scheduled to increase by a third while her salary remained the same. What angered her more was that her rent was not commensurate with the quality of her apartment.

However, she added, "I'm better off than I was a year ago." Grateful to have a challenging job, she also had a better sense of what was going on, a better overview. As she put it, she was out of the "shock phase" and able to see events more realistically. She was trying to work through in her own mind why socialism had failed and, more specifically, what she had done wrong. Such self-reflection she claimed had been absent with socialism.

Tina F.,

fifty, urban planner, formerly at the Institute for Urban Planning (*Institut für Städtebau und Architektur in der Bauakademie der* DDR)

January 1991

In all areas of life, Tina F. asserted, women came second in the GDR, including city planning. She chided the city architects for excluding women from their designs. Not only were cities planned, built, and administered by men, but "women and the city" had never even been a topic of discussion in the GDR. Many women with small children were isolated in the huge apartment complexes constructed at the city outskirts. Having stayed at home with small children herself, she knew that no structures existed to facilitate contact among the residents. "Women weren't really members of the society," she said. With the Wende *she saw the possibility of developing city spaces that would take into account the needs of women.*

A citizen of the Soviet Union, Tina F. had come to the GDR in 1963 expecting to find "the Golden West" and was disappointed to discover a country still in shambles from the war. However, she had decided to stay in the GDR and over time had become a recognized spokeswoman for women's rights and the rights of foreigners. In the fall of 1989 she supported the notion of a new democratic state and was devastated by the opening of the border on November 9: "It was like a knife in the chest." For her it meant that the independence of the GDR had been lost. Her love for her adopted country was strong, and the failure to make it better a bitter disappointment.

Tina F.

I come from the northwestern part of the Soviet Union, formerly Finnish territory. During my student years in urban planning I met a man from the GDR, and we got married and came here in the early sixties. I had to completely rethink my world when I came here from the Soviet Union. Having just left a colorful, engaged life at the university, I had an international perspective, and suddenly I came to a very small town and almost suffocated because of the provincialism. I was horrified. How could people in the middle of Europe think so provincially? At the beginning I lived with my husband's parents in two rooms with no bath, no toilet, just a single living room and a single bedroom for four people. I lived and worked under these conditions for a year. The cities, especially the city centers, were in desolate condition. From what people had told me, I had imagined I was coming to the Golden West, with modern buildings and street cars, and I was completely horrified at the war damage that was still visible not only in small towns but also in Berlin.

I moved with my family to Berlin and had problems finding a job. I had to learn to think differently in this city of millions which was very foreign to me. As a result of the move and the birth of my second child I was at home for a year and a half. There I was in the middle of the famous "three-K system," *Kinder, Küche, Kaufhalle* (children, kitchen, grocery store). The third "K" used to be *Kirche* (church). I was very isolated. Because of the high rate of employment among women, the only people who were at home in this new settlement were mothers with very young children or older retired people. Already at that point it struck me that there was something wrong with a society in which women were so isolated. There was no way for these women to communicate with each other, no clubs or organizations. They weren't really members of the society. When the men came home from work, they didn't necessarily want to talk about their work because they wanted to get some distance from it all. I saw this isolation of women with young children as a loss of quality of life. On the one hand, I thought it was wonderful to have children, but on the other hand it bothered me tremendously to be ignored in this way by society. Already back then I began to think about ways to break the monotony of this existence.

Since the *Wende,* life in the city has changed enormously. Instead of these gray, monotonous, empty streets there is suddenly life and color in the city. You used to be able to read the rhythm of people's lives in the city streets and spaces. In the early morning the entire city mobilized itself for work or day care or school. During the day the streets were completely empty, and then between 5:00 and 7:00 P.M. the empty streets came alive as people went home from work or went shopping. If you went to a department store at 11:00 A.M. it was almost deserted. This pattern was repeated year in and year out. In summer the city filled with tourists, but the daily life of the Berliners didn't change. After

8:00 P.M. the city was dead. In the apartment complexes lights burned, dinners were eaten, and then the television was turned on.

Now after the *Wende*, it all looks different in the city. And we know why. For one thing, there is an increase in things to buy. The "flying merchants" (*fliegende Händler*) have come from the West, and on almost every corner there is a stand where you can buy a sausage or a Turkish Döner sandwich. Earlier we urban planners said, "For heaven's sake, you can't have these stands in a well-planned city. Everything has to fit together correctly and harmoniously." All cities in the GDR reflect this concept with their monotony and their lack of variety, especially the more recently built apartment houses and shopping areas. And now on every street corner we have these stands. You can argue whether this is a good thing—whether they fit the image of the city—but they do provide life. There is now a great variety of things to look at and buy, and there are also more people on the streets. Of course, the other reason for the increased life on the streets is unemployment. This transitional period is much more complicated than I could have ever imagined.

The social policies of the GDR were oriented toward the nuclear family as the smallest unit of the society. Well-intentioned sociopolitical measures supported this family structure, including a broad network of day care facilities for children, and children were taken care of very well at school, disregarding for the moment what was actually taught. But the GDR had a very long work week, 43¾ hours. And when you stop to think that the new apartment complexes were built on the periphery of the city, and that in a large city like Berlin travel between work and home was extremely complicated, then women were most heavily burdened. Women had absolutely no time for themselves. So parent and children hardly saw each other. In all areas of life women came second. At work women had to give up top positions because they were burdened by children and housework. They had no time to improve themselves through further education or training or even to pursue their own interests. Men had time to develop themselves and to achieve success in their work. Even though equal rights were anchored in the constitution, women were never equal. Equality was present and supported in the legal system, and women had the right to a job, to equal pay, and so on, but it was never practiced. The society forgot that women had a job in addition to household and children.

A cliché of woman in a socialist society was created: a mother with at least two children, married, fully involved in her work, and "master" of it all. We were presented with this image of the socialist woman in all the media, but we never were shown how she was able to master it all. The main goal of politics for women was the successful combining of family and work. I remember in the early sixties the *Politbüro* decided that, in order to maintain the natural reproduction of the society, every family had to have 2.67 children. We laughed of course; it was absurd to set such a goal. Research projects were set up to determine, for example, which factors influence reproduction, or which jobs hinder reproduction. The goal was clearly to secure reproduction.

For a very long time the GDR was a closed space, a closed society, which was centered on itself. On the one hand I'm happy that there are so many aware women who before the *Wende* recognized women's double and triple burden and proclaimed that women have the right to determine their own lives. On the other hand, the majority of women in the GDR are very far from feminist thinking. The emphasis on work and family never allowed women time for self-examination. And then the women were overtaken by the process of unification. Because of the rapid annexation, the *Anschluss,* much of what the Autonomous Women's Association put forward was lost. The process of self-realization had just begun, and then it was snuffed out like a candle.

I also have to say that, to my amazement, even within the Women's Association there are some women who simply want to get ahead and will use their elbows if they have to. There's a certain lack of solidarity, which makes me very sad. This is another in a series of unpleasant realizations for me in this period of upheaval, and it has somewhat cooled my desire to involve myself. There is no real contact with women at the grass roots level. As a result of the four election campaigns that the GDR had to go through in the last year, a lot of time and energy was spent making our presence felt politically, and there was hardly time to carry feminist ideas into the broad base of the population. So the Autonomous Women's Association was created by predominately young women who were already involved in women's issues, and it was not a mass movement. Then a change occurred. Many women went back to their jobs and a vacuum was created.

Women have been increasingly cut out of political activities. They were virtually left out of the process that led to the German-German unification treaty. You can see this clearly in the discussion of the abortion issue, Paragraph 218. The politicians argued for months about a woman's right to determine for herself what she wanted to do with her body. Absurd. With the arrival of the market economy the first thing that the businesses and factories did away with were the day care facilities.

Of course there have been positive things. Freedom. The feeling of no longer being told what to do. The feeling of no longer being watched by the Party or being denounced by colleagues at work or neighbors across the hall. In addition, there are now many more choices. To what extent these possibilities can be realized is another issue. But just to have them is already something positive. My children will be able to determine for themselves what type of job or career they have, how they want to get involved in the society. That makes a huge difference. This self-determination strengthens your self-confidence and provides the opportunity to prove yourself and develop your creativity.

But it will be hard for the older generation, to which I belong. For women older than forty-five it will be very difficult to find another job. Since January 1, 1991, I have been unemployed. Because of my heavy involvement in the problems of foreign women I have had very little time to come to terms with my own situation. I'm a woman, I'm a foreigner with a GDR passport, and now I belong to the older generation. I've seen lots of job offers in the paper, and I've been fighting with myself. Should I get back into my field or should I continue to be socially and politically active, for example, in the Autonomous Women's Association? Or should I pursue another interest of mine, the notion of a state where women's needs are fully considered? Now that the conditions here have changed so drastically, how could city spaces be developed to include women? Women's ideas and needs were always ignored in urban planning.

Before I left my job I was working on a concept for the inclusion of women in city spaces. When I presented my ideas for this women-oriented urban planning, one of my male colleagues was surprised. "Do you really think women are so disadvantaged in our society?" he asked. I looked at him and said that our cities, the huge apartment settlements, were and still are planned, built, and administered by men. He couldn't believe I would dare to say such a thing. The subject of "women and the city" was never a topic of research in the GDR, although it has been pursued in the FRG and in other countries in the West. There is not a single residential area that was conceived, planned, and built by women with women in mind. Unfortunately I haven't been able to pursue this idea, because people are interested in simply surviving the changes in our society. Now we in the GDR are subject to a new building code, the West German building code. I'm sure that if the FRG had been taken over by the GDR instead of the other way around, we would have imposed our laws on them, as they are now doing to us.

I continued to have great respect for those people who wanted to reform this society. But during this time of tremendous upheaval I have been amazed at how many people have not changed on the inside but have changed on the outside, and how fast. Suddenly overnight these people have turned away from their socialist phrases and convictions and have embraced wholeheartedly this new market economy. For me it's proof that they never really believed what they were saying. And these are the people who have successfully elbowed their way into this new society. I think for example of the social scientists. How can they have spent years propagating and publishing socialist ideas and then suddenly overnight completely reject them in favor of unknown criteria and principles?

The worst thing is that the dream of a democratic society as we imagined it when we marched into the streets with hope in our hearts and light in our eyes on November 4, 1989, is gone. That was one of the most significant days of my life. I had never in my twenty-seven years in the GDR seen so many hopeful, beaming faces. It was indescribably beautiful. And then came November 9. It was like a knife in the chest. On the one hand, I was happy to see the joy of people who had been separated for twenty-eight years, but on the other hand, the goals of the great masses of the population crumbled that day. With the opening of the Wall, the independence of the GDR was relinquished and the voices that said "We are *one* people" drowned out those that said "We are *the* people." Even today this is tremendously painful for me. The hope was very strong that a new democratic society would be formed.

All of life is a process of development; it isn't stagnant. Life doesn't consist of only positive moments or ideals. It's a constant process of change, and we human beings are here to steer this process in a positive direction.

July 1992

The events since the Wende *had taken a toll on Tina F. "I'm in a thinking phase. Everything touches me deeply. I can't relate to my everyday routine or to politics. The renovation of my apartment feels like a demolition. Reading the paper has become an addiction, whether it's Paragraph 218, higher rents, or the war in Yugoslavia. It's just too much. The world is on fire. I'm depressed and lethargic. There's real confusion in my head, body, and soul. I'm a wreck."*

Despite everything, however, she had found an ABM position with a group of architects and sociologists who were engaging in alternative urban planning with a focus on sound ecological principles and East-West cooperation. She had continued her involvement with the Autonomous Women's Association, which she suggested was in the process of redefining itself. In October 1991 the organization met in Leipzig to decide whether to become a political party. The idea was defeated. Although she did not support the move to a political party, Tina F. worried that this once politically active group was shrinking to a club, and that some of the women working full time for the organization lacked a feminist consciousness. She observed this growing political disinterest in her own development as well: a People's Chamber (Volkskammer) candidate in the March 1990 elections on the joint Autonomous Women's Association/Greens list, she did not even vote in the local elections of May 1992. A possible reason for her growing apathy, she surmised, might be disgust with the Wendehälse, or turncoats, "those who affirm the opposite of what they believed before." Seeing in this type of person a decided malleability and willingness to conform, she understood how fascism could have come about.

Since the Wende she had traveled extensively, to Athens, Brussels, Stockholm, Strasbourg, Paris. Bothered by what she experienced as a gray city, she left Paris because she could not bear to see the social inequality and homelessness.

Ursula Sydow,

forty-seven, former editor (*Redakteurin*) at Aufbau publishing house, now working in advertising there

February 1991

Ursula Sydow lived alone with her mother in a typical Neubauwohnung *in a complex of hundreds of other identical small apartments. The living room was comfortable, and the walls were lined with books. When I commented on the pleasantness of the room, she smiled and said, "You would really like my garden on the outskirts of town."*

She was overjoyed at the Wende *and unification, but seemed particularly affected by the uncertainty that these events had brought with them and could not stop talking about her anxiety. Even after I turned off the tape recorder she continued to tell me about one incident after another that reinforced her fears.*

As the daughter of a man who had been employed in West Berlin—pejoratively called a "border-crosser"—she had experienced state-imposed impediments to her education and had to finish the last four years of high school at night. Completing the university with a degree in theater and German literature was, as she said, the realization of all her dreams. Ursula Sydow worked at the Aufbau publishing house, where she edited the literary journal, Weimarer Beiträge. *Even though she found satisfaction in her work, she suffered under the censorship restrictions that were ubiquitous in the publishing profession. In order to gain the trust of the authors with whom she worked, she gave them a glimpse of her political position which "wasn't the same as the official one."*

Like many people in the GDR, *she was indebted to the state for providing her a university degree and a stimulating job. But she was simultaneously limited by the state and forced to circumvent its policies in order to remain true to herself. Given this tension, it is understandable that Ursula Sydow was happy when the border opened. Literature had exposed her to places and ideas that were forbidden, but the*

Wende *allowed her finally to see with her own eyes the beauty of the Cathedral of Notre Dame.*

Ursula Sydow

I'm a product of this divided city. When he was a young man, my father got a job in the western part of Berlin as an auto mechanic with the Bosch company. He began working there in 1921 when there was no such thing as East and West Berlin and continued there after the War. I experienced lots of disadvantages because people like my father were considered border-crossers, and children of border-crossers weren't allowed to go to high school. Even though I was always good in school, I had no choice but to go into a training program, and I became very embittered. I learned stenography at a trade school, and everyone at the school got a job except me because I was the daughter of a border-crosser. The teachers said things to me like, "Your father works in the Wild West; what business do you have even being here?" I knew exactly what the teachers wanted to hear from me and answered accordingly, and it wasn't at all hard for me to distinguish between what was required of me at school and what we talked about at home.

Part of my father's salary was paid to him in West money so we enjoyed a certain status. As the economic difficulties got worse, I came to view it more and more as a privilege that I could take my West money and go shopping at the elitist Intershops. My childhood was also shaped by the fact that after the Wall went up, my father couldn't work in West Berlin anymore and was treated like dirt. Through my contacts at Henschel publishing house my father was able to find work as an auto mechanic, but he had to work with convicts. After work they were all herded into the lounge, surrounded by the civil military armed with their rifles, and were subjected to classes in political ideology. The workers didn't take it very seriously. Before the classes started they would shout, "Come on guys, it's time for our red light radiation treatment!" That was what they called it. My father was used to working at a well-equipped, modern, capitalist workshop, and suddenly at age fifty-six he was working with rats running around on the floor, up to his ankles in dirt. This treatment of my father, plus the fact that they sent half-literate people to our apartment in the evenings to teach us about Marxist-Leninist theory, had such a negative effect on me that I never joined the Party, which of course affected my career opportunities.

I finally did get my high school diploma by going to school at night. A year later I was taking courses in theater and German literature and got my degree in both areas. My university degree was the realization of all my dreams. I worked for seven years at Henschel doing things that weren't very satisfying, and then ten years ago I went to work at Aufbau publishing house where I edited a literary journal, the *Weimarer Beiträge.* My area was world literature, which I really enjoyed. Working with international literature opened up worlds to which I never had access in real life. Because I could always escape into these books, I never felt how narrow the GDR really was.

Aufbau is the largest of the publishers in East Germany and has rights to many important writers, including Christa Wolf, Christoph Hein, and Stefan Hermlin. We also produced books with a particular political function, which was to supply a certain image of reality that furthered the interests of the Party. But we had censorship. Aufbau was the publisher for the Party, which I actually didn't know for many years. I thought that all state-owned firms operated the way ours did. Only with the *Wende* have I learned that all of our profits were turned over directly to the Party. State and Party, power and Party were synonyms. You couldn't differentiate between the power of the state and the power of the Party. I'm still amazed that I ever got a job at the publishing house without being a member of the Party. I was the only non-Party member ever to hold the position of editor. Of course, I had to be very good at what I did and couldn't be politically discredited.

I had developed a way of working with the authors that enabled them to say what they wanted to say, but in a coded form. I began to give the authors a kind of "trust advance." I allowed them a glimpse of my political position, which of course wasn't the same as the official one, which was very risky for me, but as a result the authors trusted me.

No one's job is secure. If I am let go from Aufbau I have no idea what my future will be, and at age forty-seven that is not very pleasant. I might be able to get a job as a secretary because I can still do stenography, but unfortunately I have two degrees, and who is going to hire anyone like that? I don't know what possibilities exist for me. I've applied at SFB, a West Berlin radio station. The director of the station stated publicly at a meeting that he would not hire anyone from the former GDR, but I thought he meant he wouldn't hire anyone who had worked for East German radio or TV. So I applied and received an extremely cool rejection letter. They didn't even read my application. I've applied at two other stations. I'm trying to create a new start for myself in the area of theater, but I'm not having any success.

At the publishing house, they transferred me from one day to the next from the *Weimarer Beiträge* to a position in advertising. I have no experience with advertising, and I have no idea what I'm supposed to do. I feel very unsure about working in West Berlin because I still don't completely understand the rules of the game. I'm learning this life as if it were lessons in a textbook. For example, I don't know what marketing seminars are. I don't know what stress seminars are. I have never learned how to sell myself, but I'm trying.

I went to Bosch where my father used to work and asked about the pension for my mother. A very nice woman in the personnel office wanted to know more about me. She didn't seem important to me and so I decided I could practice making a positive impression on her. I played the role, and it worked perfectly. She promised to help me because I said that I hoped that with the collapse of our economic system I would finally be given a chance. She said, "I think you deserve a chance and since it won't come to you automatically, I'll help you." That surprised me because it was so human and not at all the picture we had been given of capitalism.

There's something very curious happening now. Those of us who never would have identified ourselves as East German citizens have come together as a result of the terrible way many of the *Wessis* are treating us. This strong differentiation between *Ossis* and *Wessis* will drive the *Ossis* to identify with each other in a way that we never did before. At work we were always told we were in a socialist competition against each other. Completely normal assignments at work were declared competitive assignments. It was nothing more than empty form, but it had to proceed according to this ritual, a ritual that was created by the Party.

There was a variation on this theme, the so-called Party Learning Year where certain documents from the history of the workers movement or the Party were read and discussed. It was considered the required political schooling, and everyone was expected to participate. But I didn't go because it always met on Monday evenings when I had my English class. Later I did participate, and the Monday night meetings turned into sessions where people vented their dissatisfaction. The Party didn't want this, so they stopped requiring that non-Party members attend. The whole GDR was full of just such rituals. Anyone who lived here had to participate in some way. You couldn't simply withdraw. Everyone had to make some kind of compromise.

Everyone had some sort of contact with the Stasi. Mine was relatively harmless. One evening the doorbell rang and two men were standing there. They said, "You're taking an English course at the community college, and we'd like to talk with you." Then they wanted information about someone which I couldn't give them because the person wasn't in my class. Then they wanted to come into the living room and I wouldn't let them. A few days later I was shopping with my mother and we came home and found the apartment had been searched. I asked my neighbor if she had seen anyone, and her kids said, yes, someone had been here who they didn't know. That was very common.

This is not the only instance I can name. A good friend of mine, a former teacher, wrote a letter to a West German newspaper about the bad economic conditions in the GDR and was convicted of espionage and agitation against the state. As a former pupil of his, I was interrogated for five hours by a military court in a private house with bars on the windows somewhere here in Berlin. I've always had a very good memory and so I knew exactly what I had said at the beginning of the interrogation and knew they were lying when they said, "You didn't say that before; please correct what you said." I was very young at the time and it was a horrible experience for me.

I was the only person to emerge from this trial unscathed. I decided that I didn't have to prove my I.Q. to the state security and so I played the part of a young innocent girl who had fallen in love with her teacher. I said, "What? He told political jokes? Not to us. He recited poetry, and I admired him so much." I wanted them to think I was completely stupid, and it worked perfectly. When they wanted to know about very specific political things, I said, "He didn't talk about things like that. That was beneath his dignity; we talked about literature." So I didn't hurt him. When the judge asked the prosecutor if he wanted to have me put under oath, he thought I was so dumb it wasn't worth it. The state security was the darkest thing that this society brought forth.

Actually I did have some political difficulties. In the summer of 1989 I prepared an issue of the journal on Soviet literature, which was very controversial because the GDR had not responded at all positively to *perestroika*. I included in the issue a round-table discussion of literary texts with the leading literary critics of the GDR because I thought this way no one could point the finger at any one individual: the opinions were those of a group of critics. The issue was published, which was a real accomplishment. In another case I put together two issues in one year, one on French literature and the other on U.S. literature, which were praised to the skies until the annual conference with the Central Committee. The woman representing the Party complained that the year's journals paid too much attention to Western literature. It was only two volumes out of a total of twelve, but I never heard praise again after that. I was afraid my life would continue in this same uniform, prescribed pattern, that there would be no more surprises in my life.

For this reason the *Wende* meant a great deal to me. When I heard that the Wall was open I sat here with tears streaming down my face and couldn't stop. I called a friend of mine who wasn't as excited as I was, and she couldn't understand my reaction because she had been allowed to travel, whereas I hadn't. The next day I stood in line for four hours at the police station to get a visa to cross, and then someone yelled out of the second floor window, "There aren't any more visas, we'll just stamp your identification cards." There were so many people there—estimates put the figure at about five thousand—that finally the police had people throw their I.D. cards, these very important documents, into plastic bags which were carried into the police station. Every once in a while someone gave me a sip of hot tea. At one point I had to go to the bathroom, so I jumped into my Trabant and drove home and came back as fast as I could. People asked, "How could you just leave? Your name could have been called!" Finally my name was called, and I had my stamp. But then I didn't cross. Suddenly I was afraid of this foreign city. I had to talk myself into going. We had grown up in a cage and didn't know how to deal with freedom.

A French woman I had met in 1968 when she was here for a summer course called and invited me to come visit her in Paris. So I joined the masses standing in line at the French embassy to get a visa. Then I spent three wonderful weeks in Paris. As a result of all this, it became clear to me what an incredible crime the state had committed against us by never letting us travel. I stood in the cathedral at Notre Dame with tears in my eyes and could hardly believe that I was actually seeing such beauty.

I'm not married and have no children, so I could devote all my time to my work. I never felt disadvantaged as a woman. I think women in the GDR had a lot of self-confidence. Also more and more women worked and achieved positions of relative respect. Some men had a hard time dealing with these self-confident women because they were absolutely independent.

Since the *Wende* lots of people have been talking about guilt and innocence, and I have to admit I'm not totally free of guilt, even though I have a lot less to feel guilty about than people who belonged to the Party. But even so, I went along with certain things or said nothing in certain circumstances. But it was hard to do anything else. I'm not a hero, and I've never had the ambition to be particularly brave. I was the well-behaved average citizen. Right now we're in a transition period. But I know I can't think only about myself and forget about what's going on around me. I don't want to sink into indifference. That's all I can say right now.

July 1992

In the process of the privatization of Aufbau publishing house, Ursula Sydow was tossed about from one department to another. During one of the several waves of termination, she lost her job in advertising. After learning from a West German lawyer that she had a right to six months' notification, she took legal action and was reinstated. The chaos surrounding the employment situation at Aufbau had, in her view, worsened considerably in the last year. The previous 180 employees had been reduced to 30. Having recently rejected the offer to work as a receptionist there, she preferred instead to fill in for people on vacation. She described one of her new bosses as a "yuppie Wessi who thinks we're all stupid." At the time of the interview, she thought that Aufbau would be acquired by a West German investor who wanted neither the buildings nor the land they stood on, only the publishing rights for the remaining authors. By the end of the summer, however, this offer had been rejected, which prolonged her uncertainty. When there was no longer a position for her at Aufbau, Ursula Sydow intended to apply for a job with the commission overseeing the Stasi files because, as she smirked: "They are the only ones hiring."

The turmoil of the last two years understandably led Ursula Sydow to anger and bitterness. She had to force herself to listen to the news. She had even lost the desire to read books. Her one remaining interest was travel. Wanting to make sure that I knew she was not the only one feeling this way, she quoted two obituary notices from a recent newspaper: "Freed from the fear of the future," and "His heart broke from the coldness of these times." Resigned, she felt too old to effect any change. Even the garden plot on the outskirts of town, which she called the garden of her childhood, had recently come to represent a piece of property that she owned and could sell if she had to.

Haiderun Lindner,

forty-eight, physician and mental health therapist

February 1991

When the Wall went up in August 1961, seventeen-year-old Haiderun Lindner made a conscious decision to embrace the notion that the world could be changed, and that, if practiced the way it should be, socialism could contribute to the change. She saw the Wall as a challenge, not as a barrier. Thirty years later, after disillusionment with the medical profession and harassment by the Stasi, she began to see more clearly the ways in which the SED-state's brand of socialism had affected its citizens. She seemed to take it for granted that one could not understand the significance of the recent historical events without considering the emotional experiences of the people who were involved in them.

Early in her medical career, Haiderun Lindner noticed that many of her patients were exhibiting symptoms that had no organic cause. In the 1980s she became involved in psychotherapy, despite official devaluation of the field. This training helped her observe the starkly contrasting reactions to the upheaval surrounding the Wende. Many of her patients felt a sense of worthlessness and guilt: they were being told that the failures of the forty years of the GDR were their fault, and they accepted that blame. One patient who had worked for the Stasi told her that what he saw as the heartless and ruthless treatment of East Germans by the capitalist West had relieved him of any sense of wrongdoing. In fact, he felt vindicated: socialism was indeed the more humane system.

If Haiderun Lindner was skilled in observing her patients, she scrutinized herself as well, and her self-examination turned up a certain indecisiveness with regard to the open border. The western half of the united city was for her both attractive and oppressive: on the one hand, she felt drawn to the new half of Berlin, although she found herself unable to take it all in. On the other hand, she felt free to move about the eastern part of the city.

At the time of the interview, she had already taken active measures to integrate herself into the new capitalist economy. Shortly after the Wende *she had persuaded a number of other doctors to open a joint practice. But the venture was being hampered by the issue of western ownership of the building in which the office was located. Still, it was clear that Haiderun Lindner would be able to ride out the change very well.*

Haiderun Lindner

My strongest childhood memories had to do with fascism. In the 1950s we were constantly confronted with films about Auschwitz, and all I knew was that I didn't want to be like those people: don't go along, don't accommodate. I remember a meeting with the higher-ups in the FDJ that reminded me of what I had seen in the films about fascism: what was important was following orders; the individual didn't count. My mother always said they had learned everything from the Nazis: the parades, the torchlight demonstrations, the empty phrases. Of course I was in the FDJ myself. That didn't mean anything. We were all in the FDJ, but I never joined the Party.

My parents weren't political, and I wasn't either, but I was strongly influenced by Bertolt Brecht who was more an intellectual than a state poet and whose sense of social justice coincided with mine. I read everything he wrote and saw his plays twice a week at the Berliner Ensemble. I acted sometimes in a workers' theater and found that literature made my life interesting. When I was sixteen or seventeen I wanted to do something with literature and decided to be an actress. I applied at a few places, but nothing came of it. We were always told we should do something useful for the state which made me feel guilty, so after I got out of high school I did a year of practical work, a half year making metal parts on a machine in a factory, and a half year in a hospital. But it turned out that I wasn't very good at these things, and a friend of mine suggested that I study medicine. She said I could help people that way. That was 1961.

When the Wall appeared on August 13 of that same year, my solution to the problem was Brecht, something intellectual, an ideal. I embraced the idea that the world could really be changed. I decided that socialism wasn't bad, and, if done right, it could be something good. So I consciously decided not to get upset about the Wall and instead to take it as a challenge. This attitude was quickly corrected when I was required to sign an oath of loyalty to the state in medical school. At that point I knew that the kind of socialism intellectuals hoped for was an illusion.

In 1968 I finished my studies and started working in Potsdam-Babelsberg. I lived in Berlin, but I went to Potsdam every day, and then traveled from factory to factory to see patients. I quit the hospital because the working conditions were so bad. I didn't want a lot of children, but I was twenty-eight when I got pregnant and I thought, if I don't have a child now things will probably continue like this and I may never have a child. I took my son to private day care for the first two years. I didn't want him to go to the state-supported nursery facility because a small child needs at least one person he can relate to. When he was three he did go to day care, which he wanted to do, and it was good for him to have the contact with other children.

After Benjamin's birth I started to get interested in the psychological side of medicine. First of all there was my own personal situation. I had been with a man for six years, and that had ended with a dramatic separation. He treated me very badly, and I wanted to get away from him. Then I met my present husband—he more or less saved me from that relationship. I began to examine myself and to ask what had caused me to get involved with a weaker man and then to be tyrannized by him. In addition to my personal situation, I noticed that many of my patients had symptoms and complaints for which there were no organic causes. Thirty to forty percent of the people who came to us weren't organically sick. I tried to empathize with these patients, but I realized fairly quickly that I could only go so far with empathy. So I started a course in psychotherapy designed for doctors.

In the early eighties I also read a lot of psychotherapy and began to understand some things about myself, my difficulties with intimacy, and so on. Then I did an additional two-year course in psychotherapy and now I do psychotherapy with my patients on a regular basis. I'm interested in creating a balance between treatment of the physical body and treatment of the psyche because the psyche has been neglected. Young medical students in their first years of medical school are interested in the psychological side of illness, but in later years they are led away from it because the professors devalue it and recommend instead a specialty in surgery or something connected with high technology, the areas which have the least to do with the human being. Psychotherapists in the GDR who went into this area did so against the generally approved opinions and attitudes. Freud was not to be read, psychoanalysis was bourgeois. Of course, we read Freud and studied psychoanalysis anyway, but in order not to frighten the higher-ups we called it "dynamic therapy."

We had one purpose, and that was to overthrow authority. The members of the group learned how to overthrow the leader, the father figure, who for his part frustrated and agitated the group. This process mirrored what happened in the greater society. You were supposed to defend yourself, make yourself autonomous, recognize your own potential, and come to terms with your superiors from a position of strength. It was a little bit like educating people to revolution. People have psychological problems everywhere in the world, but in the GDR people felt more pressure and compulsion. People thought they had to adapt to authority. They thought everything was their own fault. The problem with doing this work was that the people who had developed a different consciousness were released into a world that didn't reward their new thinking.

The *Wende* brought tremendous change into the lives of my patients. It was like an earthquake. Virtually everyone has been uprooted and feels his or her life threatened in some way, whether ideologically or economically. No one knows how much the rent will be raised by the end of the year. A good half of my patients are already unemployed. I'm surprised that they are taking it all so quietly and with such a sense of guilt. There's a lot of depression and very little outrage. I'm amazed that I have to ask my patients about their present job situation. Before, they talked about their difficulties on their own. They're afraid of losing their jobs and afraid of not having enough money, and they feel incapable of dealing with the new structures that appear every day, insurance and tax forms and so on. To get an identification card as a handicapped person you have to go to at least five different locations.

People in their late forties and early fifties are the worst off because they have been fired in the greatest numbers and they won't be able to find another job. People in this age group had accomplished something in their lives, but they had also covered up the mistakes of the system. They are hearing that nothing they did was worth anything and, in addition, that it's all their fault: they tolerated the decaying state, half the people worked for the Stasi and the other half didn't work very hard. There have to be reasons why the economy fell apart. So these people have lost their jobs or expect to, and they'll never get another job where their sense of responsibility will be taken seriously; instead they are getting the blame for the rottenness of the system.

We often said that our entire economy was being supported by fifty-year-old women with varicose veins. The young women all had children and took their baby year off. Then they came back to work, and the children got sick, and they took time off again. If a department had eight people and four of them were young women with children, and two of those positions were empty because children were sick, then the whole department was maintained by the two fifty-year-old women with this strong sense of responsibility.

GDR women were in terrific shape emotionally. They had their jobs and were responsible for the family. Plus they had to be attractive. If they were intellectual they had to be able to carry on a conversation in the evening and not fall right into bed. At work they had to be as good as a man. This always made me like GDR women. I like women who are active and who I can talk to. I can reach an agreement with women more easily than with men. Women are better able to solve conflicts than men and are able to deal with much more than men. Men are more single-track and perhaps for that reason they can get their way, but they can also be more stubborn, more inhibited, more repressed. This is all right at work, but when problems arise men lose their balance more easily. Women have always had to wear many hats. They had their jobs, their family, the food shopping, their grandmother to take care of, and they also had to buy the Christmas tree. The man took care of the car.

Right now, though, both men and women are being affected. One of my female patients had a terrific anxiety attack during one of our talks, and a lot of political things came out. But at the moment nobody is talking much about the political issues because the survival issues are so great. Money has suddenly taken on a huge role. Before, money wasn't important because everyone had approximately the same small amount, or at least there weren't the huge differences in wealth that there are in the West. People have started thinking they have to save every penny. I've noticed this attitude in myself. I've stopped having my laundry done and suddenly I have mountains of sheets here in the apartment because the price has tripled from Marks 12 to DM 35. I can't plan for the future.

From a psychotherapeutic point of view, it will take two or three years to work this all through. People are only very slowly beginning to think back over what happened here. Right now I'm performing crisis intervention. The only people who are willing to really work on what's happening to them are people who have suffered an additional loss, the loss of a spouse, for example. All the others are simply holding their breath and waiting to see how much worse things are going to get.

Within the Party people are having various reactions. First, those who completely identified with the system, the ones who believed in the Party, have suffered a tremendous loss: the possibility of a utopia. Second, the honest Party members who complained and tried to improve things and were punished for it now feel they've been betrayed two and three times over. The good and loyal Party members who never deviated from the Party line, on the other hand, are now happy just to get their pension. These are the ones who accepted whatever came from above before, and now they are conforming again to what they are being told. These people aren't torn up so much inside.

I've had a couple of Stasi people as patients too. Their reactions range from repression and silence to wanting to work through their past. One of them is simply afraid. He's lonely and depressed and is afraid to say anything. Another is trying to get a job in West Berlin. He'd be happy to work as a doorman, as long as he can survive. Because of what is happening to people here, anyone who might have a guilty conscience feels cleared of any wrongdoing. They can point to the gloomiest pronouncements of the Stalinists regarding the horrors of capitalism: England in the nineteenth century, mass unemployment, and so on, and they are fully vindicated.

I was terribly harassed by the Stasi, partly because of what some of my friends had done. I knew some people who had crossed over to the West, and I had a woman friend who had been thrown in jail for a year. She lived in Weimar in a one-family house. Her sister had removed an SED campaign poster from their garden gate because she thought the Party had no business putting it in front of their house, and as a result the mother and three sisters were arrested. The state prosecutor who was supposed to take the case refused and was demoted. Then another prosecutor was put on the case, and it was made into a showpiece. So at age eighteen my friend spent a year in jail. Eight years later in 1968 she went across the border into the FRG, and I haven't heard from her since. I'll never forget what she said, though: "Everything that you say to anyone is information for the Stasi." And that's correct. I was asked several times if I would work for the Stasi. I wasn't alone. In fact I hardly know anyone who wasn't asked. I was never asked to join the Party. People who were asked worked in the ideology apparatus, such as television, the university, and so on.

If I am happy about one thing it's that there is no more Stasi. I'm sure they had a file on me, but I haven't seen it. I would certainly hope I have a file! The whole Stasi thing escalated around the business with my son. It started in September of 1988 with an antifascism demonstration at Marx-Engels Platz, when Benjamin and a few other boys went to the rally carrying signs against fascist tendencies in the GDR, against the Skinhead movement. Their signs were taken away and their names were written down, but they weren't arrested.

Then came the business at the school. Benjamin was in the twelfth grade at the Ossietzky School and was one of four students who were expelled. The school had a bulletin board where students could express their opinions. Together with the son of a friend of mine, Benjamin put up an article about the Solidarity movement in Poland and the strikes by the workers. He wrote: "Only if all democratic forces in Poland stand together will they be able to effect change." This was absolute poison to the government here. Then a friend of his put up a letter critical of the military parade planned for October 7, the national holiday, which wasn't even very negative. It simply asked a question: "Given the political movement toward peace all over the world, is it absolutely necessary that on the anniversary of our Republic tanks should roll? Couldn't the holiday be conceived differently?"

These things were seen as an attack on everything that was good and holy, and an inferno broke loose. You can't imagine. There were delegations from the FDJ leadership, from the Party, and from the highest level of the government. Egon Krenz and Secretary of Education Margot Honecker got involved because Krenz's son was at the same school. It became a state issue. Benjamin was branded the ringleader of this subversive group, which in turn of course had been "directed from the West." The boys were accused of antisocialist behavior during a horrible meeting, a kind of hearing, with twelve people made up of Stasi and the highest school officials. The point of the hearing was to bring evidence to prove that these kids had a bad attitude about their country. We had Stasi posted in front of our house whose job it was to find out who belonged to this core group. It was really awful.

The parents at the school got together and wrote letters of protest. It got into the international media, and we received letters from everywhere in the GDR and West Germany and from Holland and Sweden, from institutions, and so on. The church sponsored meetings and services. Finally it became such a hot issue that it could only really be decided by Honecker himself. Because of this international attention the sentence was mild: the boys were only expelled. But they were branded criminals. Some of the teachers behaved despicably toward them. Now those teachers have all been fired and Benjamin and the boys have been readmitted, but during the time between their expulsion and the *Wende*, I was constantly afraid. Benjamin was a bit of a radical, and he continued to be active in the peace group in Weissensee and got involved in observing the last elections before 1989. So the Stasi was always close by, always observing Benjamin.

At one of the demonstrations sponsored by the Weissensee peace group on September 7, 1989, Benjamin was baby-sitting for a friend of mine and had taken the boy to a playground. The whole time two men sat in a Wartburg ten feet away and kept their eye on this state criminal. The boy's mother went to the demonstration and was beaten so badly by the Stasi that she came to see me the next day for medical treatment. She had huge marks on her legs and arms. Another person who was arrested had a leg broken and during the four hours of questioning wasn't allowed to see a doctor.

My husband was warned by the Interior Ministry to stop our activities. I had the clear impression that if, for example, we had gone on West German television we probably would have been brought to trial for subversive activity and then gotten kicked out, and I didn't want to leave this country. Somehow I love the people here and I like a lot of things about the GDR. I said to myself, this isn't Mr. Krenz's country; it's my country.

When November 9 came, I couldn't believe it. Even today when I walk along places where the Wall used to be I'm overwhelmed. The streets that used to end at the Wall simply continue into the West. Every time I see it, it makes me cry. People made jokes about everything, but not about the Wall. When I was in West Berlin three years ago I was completely enchanted by the paintings on the West side of the Wall: the paintings made the Wall disappear. I went with friends to Potsdamer Platz which I can remember seeing as a small girl. After the war there wasn't much to see anyway, mostly stands and booths where people were selling things. But when I saw Potsdamer Platz from the West side I began to cry. What had our government done to this beautiful city? This huge dead space had become a symbol of a living thing that had been ripped apart.

Unfortunately I haven't had time during this turbulent year to really absorb the new city. It is still very foreign to me. When I go over they notice I'm from the East, and then when I come back here I can hardly look at our broken-down houses. But I also feel I can move freely again. I have this contradictory relationship with the whole thing. It's both attractive and oppressive.

I've decided to continue to work as a doctor. It was clear already a year ago that the system from West Germany would be imposed here. So I said, look, we can only survive if we create a joint practice. We have an eye doctor, a gynecologist, and a few others. The building we're in belongs to someone in the West, or rather, it belongs to a community of heirs, and no one knows who they all are.

We know one of them, but she doesn't have a certificate of heirship so we can't get a rental contract for our offices. We've hired a lawyer, and he's been corresponding with lawyers in the West and with the former housing authorities here in the East. I'll probably earn less at the beginning than the nurse I've hired and won't be able to take any vacations for a while, but hopefully things will improve in the next few years.

No one is working through what really happened. Nothing is being published here about how things really stood with the Stasi or with the economy. How were things done? How many people's lives were torn to shreds? All this is being pushed aside with the accusation, "You stupid *Ossis*, you went along with all this." And no one here is asking, how could I have allowed them to do this to me? No one is saying, I'm proud of what I was able to accomplish here.

The worst thing is this desire not to talk about it. It would be terrible if we repeated our experience after World War II. I always asked my mother how it was back then, whether there were any Jews where we lived in Kleinmachnow, how such things could happen. My mother avoided my questions and said, "No, we didn't have any Jews. I never knew any. I only heard about some Jews who had a store and then they somehow left." I asked, "Where did they go, and didn't you do anything?" and she said, "You weren't allowed to say anything." Our parents were all much less political than we were here, but they dismissed the past. They said it was all stupid, or it wasn't really so bad. It would be awful if that were to happen again.

July 1992

When I walked into Haiderun Lindner's office for our second interview, the success of her private practice was readily apparent. Fresh paint and new furniture had brought noticeable changes, and although the ownership question remained unresolved, her practice continued to expand. "I've become a businesswoman," she said. "I work twelve to fourteen hours a day and attend seminars on weekends." She was clearly pleased with the way things were going for her professionally.

She had overcome her own anxiety about establishing an independent practice, but she had noticed that her patients' fears had worsened. Unemployment was up—particularly among people who had had good jobs—and pensions weren't keeping pace with rising rents. People with good pensions, however, were less anxious. She suggested that these people had real reason to ask themselves what they had done in the SED-state, but—perhaps because they were financially se-

cure—they did not seem to care. She respected those who were asking themselves about their own involvement and mentioned Jutta Braband who had publicly acknowledged her Stasi past: "What more could you want than someone who changed her mind and distanced herself from the Stasi years before it became a public issue."

Jutta Braband,

forty-one, representative of the
United Left (*Vereinigte Linke*) to the
Bundestag from the state of
Brandenburg

February 1991

Jutta Braband was an active member of the political opposition in the GDR. *Along
with others who in the fall of 1989 created the prodemocracy group United Left
(*Vereinigte Linke*) she believed in the ideal of a socialist democracy. She had tried
to bring troubling issues to the attention of the* SED-*state by participating in
demonstrations and circulating letters of protest. She cried the night the Wall
opened because without the border, she feared the goal of a democratic* GDR, *which
she and her friends had fought for, could no longer be realized.*

*Despite her experience in the opposition, however, Jutta Braband questioned the
appropriateness of the term "dictatorship" when applied to the* GDR. *Acknowledg-
ing that many laws oppressed East Germans, she nonetheless commended the state
for allowing its citizens to push against the limits of the law. She pointed out that
laws were enforced differently in the* GDR *than in oppressive countries such as
South Africa or Chile: "The* GDR *at least attempted to maintain the appearance of
a state based on law."*

*Jutta Braband's story is striking because it describes the path from opposition
leader and political outsider in the* GDR *to political participation within the new
united Germany as* Bundestag *representative for the state of Brandenburg. Moreover, her story illuminates the uncertainties and difficulties which unification
brought to the* Bundestag.

When I spoke with Jutta Braband, the all-German Bundestag *had been in
session only two months. She told of the boos and whistles that interrupted the*
Bundestag *speeches of well-known East Germans like Hans Modrow and* PDS-
*head Gregor Gysi. She talked about the disdain felt by West German representa-
tives for all members of the* Bundestag *who could be identified with the* SED-*state.*

She saw this disdain as evidence of the "simplistic black-and-white thinking" which did not differentiate between East Germans who supported the state and those who tried to reform it.

Her desire for "radical democracy" she said differed significantly from the "bourgeois parliamentarianism" she experienced in the Bundestag: *"A society can't exist on the basis of a majority and a minority but has to recognize that many different minorities exist, many different groups with different interests." Remembering the Berlin Round Table where she represented the United Left and where every representative participated in trying to reach consensus, she longed for a more egalitarian democracy than was practiced in the* Bundestag.

In spite of her disillusionment with the workings of the federal Parliament, Jutta Braband nevertheless realized that change was possible in the new Federal Republic, if by different means than she had anticipated: "I don't believe that I'll change anything [by my work in the Bundestag*]. What I do believe is that I can make things public. Changing the system requires education."*

Jutta Braband

In 1979, nine well-known writers were thrown out of the state Writers' Association, the *Schriftstellerverband,* among them Stefan Heym, because they had criticized the cultural politics of the leadership in the GDR. The opposition peace group to which I belonged wrote a letter to the Party leadership protesting the expulsion because it was the equivalent to forbidding these writers to work. It was an opportunity for us to protest the kind of political actions that occurred every day in the GDR. After the letter, the state tried to criminalize us, but they weren't successful until finally a stranger brought us some magazines from South America. He put the magazines in a locker at the train station as a ploy, and when I went to pick them up I was arrested because it was forbidden to read materials from the West. I'm sure he was an undercover agent for the state. The secret police didn't want people in the opposition to meet and do things together. That was normally severely punished. We actually got a light sentence, but on the other hand we really hadn't done anything very serious.

I was imprisoned for nine months. It was horrible. I know now that I had never experienced loneliness before that, and I will never forget how it felt. For seven months I was in pretrial detention, but these months were counted as part of my punishment, so when my case came up my sentence was almost complete. The detention center was under the supervision of the Stasi and, as far as material conditions were concerned, it was one of the best supplied and equipped. The food was relatively good.We could shower once a week, and once a week a book cart came by and everyone was given two books.

I was in a room with a thick steel door that had a small window. In pretrial detention we weren't supposed to come in contact with other people because maybe we would doctor up our story. So I was isolated. There were ten separate cells or walkways in the courtyard where each of the ten prisoners could go to get fresh air. I never saw anyone else. After sentencing, I was placed in a real prison where conditions were different. I had the right to have visitors, to watch television, and to work. I can understand how important work was. What were we supposed to do all day? We weren't allowed to work while we were in pretrial detention. That was a time where we were supposed to turn inward and realize we had done something wrong. It was supposed to be a kind of punishment, I suppose. After seven months I simply couldn't read any more, so I carried on long conversations in my head with Christa Wolf.

Our trial was quite remarkable. Normally such trials were closed to the public, but this trial was open. The room was extremely small, and it was already full with Thomas and me, the defending attorney, the prosecutor, and the judge. Our lawyer had managed to get permission for my sister and Thomas's mother to participate in the trial. Many of our friends stood outside the courtroom and couldn't get in. The sentences that were handed down by the judge were lower than what the prosecuting attorney had asked for. That was very unusual.

And still another unusual thing about this trial was that our attorney made a motion for acquittal. That simply wasn't done in the GDR, not in political trials. Political trials were programmed. You knew that the accused would be found guilty. If a defending attorney dared to move for acquittal he had to be crazy or tired of living, because it was very probable that he would get into trouble. But our attorney was able to support his motion extremely well, and besides we had the best lawyer in the GDR, Gregor Gysi. Gysi was always getting into trouble, but he was very strong and had a remarkable imagination. I have seldom known anyone who knew the law so well and was able to exhaust all the possibilities of the law. When he said certain things during the trial, I thought he was going to end up in jail himself, but people with legal training had to admit that he was right.

I'm not a philosopher, but when people say we had a dictatorship here I have to say there's a significant difference between what went on in countries like

Chile or South Africa or Turkey, and what went on in the GDR. The GDR at least attempted to maintain the appearance of a state based on law. In part the state made its laws in such a way that it was able to oppress people, but it also tried to uphold these laws. If you acted within and up to the limits of the law you could accomplish much more than normal people ever thought was possible. Most people never even tried. A state which tries to uphold its laws has to give people who turn against the state the opportunity to defend themselves against the state. And Gysi was excellent. He didn't tell the judge to be nice to us because we were young and didn't know what we were doing. He said we had the right to do what we did. There's a tremendous difference between the two arguments.

After I was released from prison I think I was unconsciously afraid of getting arrested again and so I moved a little bit more cautiously than before. My friend Thomas Klein kept me from taking part in certain activities because he was afraid for me. For example, the protest activities surrounding Chernobyl. I said, "I'm sorry, I won't stay in the background any longer. I have to do what I think is right, and I'm going to go out and gather signatures. After Chernobyl we circulated a protest letter describing the dangers of atomic energy and demanding that the GDR stop building atomic reactors. We tried to bring the issue into the open because most problematic things here were never discussed openly. These protest letters were sent to the Party leadership or to Honecker himself. We tried to document that there were lots of people in the country who had different opinions from the officially sanctioned ones.

We also divided the work up among us. When you work illegally as we did, there were always some people who planned the activities, others who participated in them, and others who acted as hiding places. I was a hiding place. I hid a computer and a printer. People like me who have been in jail normally don't take part in activities or go to illegal meetings because the danger of getting caught is too great. I had my place in the scheme of things. After prison I wasn't on the front lines, but I was a part of things. We changed functions from time to time.

Other activities of the opposition included building a human chain that was to go between the American and Soviet embassies [to protest the arms race]. The Stasi found out about it, but they handled it in such an elegant way that I actually had to admire them. It was really impressive. In order to prevent them from demonstrating, the Stasi picked up thousands of people from work and drove them home or went shopping with them. They didn't arrest them. The women Stasi were the most imaginative. They got into the people's cars and had themselves driven around town. They picked up their laundry, went to the market to buy what they needed for dinner that night, picked up their children.

The opposition in the GDR was quite leftist. It didn't call itself leftist, but its goals were what are commonly called leftist. We didn't talk about communism or socialism, we talked about democracy. But it was a radical kind of democracy [where all issues would be decided by direct vote], not a bourgeois parliamentarianism [where voters elect representatives to vote on issues for them]. We wanted free elections but not with the results that we got. That goes against everything we stood for. When you look at the neo-Nazis and Skinheads here in the former GDR you can see there was also a kind of opposition on the right.

For many years before the *Wende,* many small groups formed what we call circle groups, where people came together to read something or to learn something. There was no unified opposition movement, only these small peace groups. Then in 1989 the mood in the country was such that something had to happen. People from the small groups tried to do something and founded the various currents of the citizens' movement. Some friends of mine and I started the United Left, Bärbel Bohley and a few of her friends formed New Forum, and Lotte Templin and her husband started Initiative for Peace and Human Rights. The peace groups that had worked together for the previous twelve years formed the basis for the citizens' movement. All the people who had leadership positions in the citizens' movement knew each other and had worked with each other for many years. It was like a big family.

The psychological breaking point occurred around October 7, 1989. A huge number of people had left the GDR through the open Hungarian border. Parents, children, women, men, single mothers, everyone was affected by the wave, and so there was a tremendous sadness in the country. The people who stayed felt completely helpless. This sadness slowly turned to anger which broke out on October 7, the national holiday. On that day people who had allowed things to go along as they always had, people who always managed to justify things that weren't right, who always said that because the larger goal was the good of all people, it was necessary to bear the problems of the present, those people finally woke up.

Two months later, in December, the Round Table was set up. When historians look back on that time I think they'll say it was a time of government on two levels. Hans Modrow was the new head of government and he tried to ignore the Round Table. He visited it, but that was all. By the end of January he realized that he couldn't govern without including it. The security police was being dissolved, and there were huge protests. The anger was directed against the Party leadership and the Stasi. It was a tremendously explosive situation, and there could have been civil war in the country. I think it was a shock for some to discover that the people in the Party leadership had lived like gods, although I think their standard of living was actually more bourgeois. At first I was angry at the people for being so disappointed, and later I understood that people had taken what the leadership said seriously—that we were all equals. At least the huge disparity in wealth that exists in West Germany or the United States didn't exist here.

So I was a representative of the United Left at the Round Table, which was perhaps the most positive experience for me of the past year. Depending on the topic to be discussed, different people were there, people who had a particular knowledge of the subject. We didn't operate on the basis of representative parliamentarianism, but rather sent people to the Round Table who knew what they were talking about. There were a number of people who represented the United Left on a rotating basis. One of the most important experiences of this period was the attempt to reach consensus. This experience increased in importance after the *Volkskammer* elections on March 18, 1990, and has become much more important to me now that I'm in the *Bundestag*. In the *Bundestag* there is absolutely no attempt to reach consensus. Everything is clearly defined, the majority is fixed, and there is no attempt to come together. There's a lot of discussion for the sake of the public, but that's all it is. That's demoralizing. Now I understand why so few people want to get involved in politics. There's no point. I think we need to find other methods.

The Round Table was an outline for the future. It represented the idea that a society can't exist on the basis of a majority and a minority, but has to recognize that many different minorities exist, many different groups with different interests who can sit at one table and try to reach agreement with each other. In the private sphere it is possible for people who represent different interests to come together. I think it must be possible on a public scale. Lots of people say this is an illusion and I'm idealistic, but I don't agree. If it can function in a family, it can function in a society, although I realize that it's much more difficult. So the experience at the Round Table was very important for me: people with different interests sat at one table and were all equal. If I hadn't had this experience, I might think that it was illusory, but I had it and it worked. And there was no civil war in the GDR. The Round Table managed to bring something forward.

The fact that something entirely different resulted, something which I didn't want, is another story.

I also ran as a candidate for the *Volkskammer* in the elections of March 18. I always considered politics dirty, but I didn't think I could look my children in the eyes if I didn't run. It's not honest to talk about something all the time and then not to do anything about it. But I didn't win. There was one seat for the United Left, and my friend Thomas Klein, who was in prison with me, got it. Then I campaigned for a seat in the *Bundestag* because I did not agree with what was happening in the spring of 1990. And I thought it was important for people to be elected to the *Bundestag* who at least could remember what it was they wanted for the future. The GDR existed for forty years, but it wasn't all bad, and it stood for an ideal which not only people on the left believed in. I thought that the first all-German *Bundestag* had to have people in it who carried this ideal forward. It would have been unbearable without such people.

It's actually unbearable as it is. The *Ossis,* those of us from the East, are only identifiable as such in two parties, the two parties made up entirely of people from the East: the Coalition 90/Greens, which is primarily people from the democracy movement, and the PDS/United Left. In the other parties you can't tell who the *Ossis* are, but I've heard that the people from the East are having a hard time with their Western party colleagues because they feel inferior. They're treated badly. I recently made a speech in the *Bundestag* on the environment and was told I was responsible for forty years of bad economics in the GDR. People don't differentiate. People know I'm from the East but don't know that I'm not a member of the PDS. I got elected through the United Left, which started working with the PDS after the election. When Hans Modrow goes to the podium they start shouting at him immediately, or Gregor Gysi. That is simplistic black-and-white thinking: SED is the same as PDS is the same as Stasi.

The TV camera that shoots the *Bundestag* meetings regularly takes shots that exclude the PDS/United Left. When we're scheduled to speak, our speeches aren't carried on TV because they're always scheduled for the time after the cameras have left at 4:00 in the afternoon. The meetings often go until 10:00 or 11:00, and our times are always at the end. In their desperation to be heard, the Coalition 90 recently attacked the PDS/United Left, which was really terrible. The people from the PDS who are in the *Bundestag* are not the ones responsible for the wrongs of the past. In many cases the PDS people who were members of the old SED belonged to the so-called reform wing of the Party. These people can't be made responsible for everything that happened, and yet they bear some responsibility. But the people in Coalition 90 aren't going to create opportunities for coming to terms with the past by pointing their finger at us. It will only deepen the cleft between us. The absurd thing is that we have the same goals.

Some people think it's terrible that I am associated with the PDS. I think this will change. I hope it will. I went into the *Bundestag* because my vote represents a broad alliance of the left, not left in the sense of communist. Lots of people have different words for it: alternative, feminist, ecological, radical democratic. These people have a similar point of departure, and I think these people should work together.

As far as women in the *Bundestag* are concerned, there are some strong women, for example, in the SPD. We have four women who want to create some alternatives for women, but there are also some women in the PDS who haven't thought about these issues. Relatively few West German women have positions in the political arena, whereas here it's the other way around. It was taken for granted that there would be a 50 percent representation of women in the PDS, although there was some argument about it, which was ridiculous because the PDS has more women than men anyway.

Political activity in the *Bundestag* with regard to women's issues presently consists of trying to maintain in the new unified Germany what we had in the GDR. That's not progress. I hoped to be able to move former GDR women forward because women were oppressed even though they had lots of advantages. Even with the same education or training as men, even with salaries that were almost the same as men's, they were never exactly the same; and even with day care facilities, all of this didn't add up to equality. While women in the West were fighting for equal rights, we wanted equal status because we knew from experience that having equal rights isn't enough. Real equal opportunity is what's important, not the fact that some law states that I have equal rights. If in reality the man is always preferred over me, then I don't have a chance.

In general I have the distinct impression that the clock is being turned back. More than half of the unemployed here in the former GDR are women, of course, once again. They're supposed to stay at home and take care of their children because there isn't enough money to maintain the day care facilities. In the GDR 92 percent of women worked, and the vast majority enjoyed it. It was normal and taken for granted that every girl learned a trade or a profession and then practiced it. Maybe it's true that women here don't appear to be as modern as women in the West. They're not as open or relaxed. Our women looked like "mommies." No one would have guessed that behind that exterior there was a self-confident, robust, active, woman.

I have tremendous difficulties combining my job at the *Bundestag* with my duties in the family. I constantly feel guilty. I don't have time to clean the house or really attend to my seven-year-old son. When I come home after three or four days in Bonn, he won't leave me alone. In addition to my political activities, I also have a real career. I'm a fashion designer, and I love it. And that's another problem. I want to be able to do everything and know that I can't.

On the other hand, in a certain way I don't take my work in the *Bundestag* seriously. I have a different notion of democracy than what is practiced in the *Bundestag*. I will try to accomplish what I can, but I won't put all my energy into this work. I don't believe that I'll change anything. What I do believe is that I can make things public. Changing the system requires education.

The loss of the GDR will have terrible consequences on a social level. In West Germany there were two forces at work for the public good: the trade unions with their fight for salaries and benefits, and the existence of the GDR. West Germany was always looking over its shoulder to see what we in the GDR were able to achieve in the area of social benefits and tried to keep up with us wherever they could. What impressed and motivated the West German government were the year of paid leave for either parent, the availability of inexpensive day care, the educational opportunities, and all the facilities for women. These conditions always served as a kind of example for the trade union movement in West Germany, and now they're gone.

The radical changes in the GDR affected me also on a personal level. On October 2, 1989, my daughter left the GDR and went to the West German embassy in Prague to try to get to the West. She hadn't come home for days, and when a friend of hers made a telling comment, I went into her room and looked in her closet and saw that an entire shelf was empty. Then I called all her friends; none of them was home. One of their mothers asked me, don't you know? They're all sitting in the embassy. I thought about it all for a day and realized she hadn't said goodbye to me, so I went to Prague and saw her there along with the six thousand other people. It was as if I had been struck by lightning. I couldn't comprehend it. I watched her at the embassy and could see that she was the weak link in the chain, but I didn't make the least effort to keep her from leaving. It hurt me terribly, but I thought she had to make the decision for herself. She never shared my ideas and I don't think she was ever at a meeting where I made a speech. She just wasn't interested. It wasn't as though I only discovered this there in the embassy grounds in Prague, but there it became manifest. I felt a bit betrayed, but I also knew I couldn't do anything. She was one of the first to leave the embassy and go to the West, to friends in Munich. But she didn't stay there long. She went to West Berlin and then to the United States and then came running back home.

On November 9 I cried, not for joy that the border was open, but because I had a strong feeling that everything was over. I thought, with the border gone nothing we wanted will be possible. People will throw themselves into what's easy and available and will no longer do what's difficult. I never thought about unification, not in my wildest dreams. I know that it was a mistake not to think about it. But we didn't care about the other German state. It was never our goal. We simply underestimated what was going on. When I saw how many people from East Berlin cried when they saw a certain street or because they now could visit certain people, only then did I realize what a mistake we had made. I never left the GDR, even though it was bad, because I wanted something different for it. This something different wasn't the Federal Republic.

July 1992

Jutta Braband could not be reached for a second interview. However, some of the changes that occurred for her in the period since our first conversation became public in essays she wrote for the German press, including "The White Spot on My Black Vest," (Neues Deutschland, September 18, 1991) and "Jutta Braband on the Resignation of Her Position as Bundestag Representative after Examination by the Stasi-Commission" (Neues Deutschland, February 21, 1992). A shorter version of the latter article appeared in Die Zeit (March 6, 1992, overseas edition) under the title "Why Was I Silent So Long?" In place of a second interview, we have drawn from these essays to update her story.

In "The White Spot on My Black Vest," Jutta Braband voluntarily disclosed her involvement as an "informal collaborator" (Inoffizielle Mitarbeiterin) with the GDR state security because she wanted to encourage discussion of a complex and sensitive issue which, she wrote, many would rather ignore. She argued for a differentiated approach to the GDR past, urging an open and honest discussion of all levels of Stasi involvement, beginning with her own. Particularly in the latter essay, she criticized the black-and-white thinking that categorically condemned all those who worked for the Stasi without regard for such factors as the manner in which they were recruited, the length of their service, what they actually did for the Stasi, and what motivated them to break their contact. She also emphasized the importance of evaluating a person's political activity in the years following any association with the Stasi.

How was it possible for Jutta Braband to become engaged with the state security? The story of her involvement—told in the first article—began with her unshakable belief in the socialist ideal. The political fervor she showed in high school brought recruiters from the Stasi to her apartment when she was only twenty-one years old. They promised to help her realize this ideal if she would give them information about people at her workplace. She agreed to cooperate with the state security, thinking the information she passed on would be helpful to the state she believed in.

The man she called her Stasi-father gained her trust by taking her political questions seriously—something that had hardly been possible elsewhere. He convinced her that she was needed to help "fight the enemy from the FRG and the USA," a notion that coincided with her own convictions. For her, "anything was better than capitalism." Then in her mid-twenties, she became friends with people who were also committed to the socialist ideal but did not believe that it could be realized from within the SED-state. They argued that the system itself needed to be changed. These friends helped her see her role in perpetuating the system. They convinced her that "day after day thousands of people allowed themselves to be controlled with the excuse of fighting the 'enemy of the state.'"

When she talked to her Stasi-father about these criticisms as well as the oppression that her friends were experiencing at the hands of the state security, his explanations sounded increasingly hollow. She began to question seriously her connection with the Stasi. Furthermore, because her circle of friends consisted solely of people who opposed the state, she realized that any information she passed on would have to involve those closest to her. She found the courage to tell her Stasi-father that she disagreed with the state's methods of achieving real socialism and therefore saw no reason to continue their conversations. This was a difficult and courageous step since she now realized that her once congenial relationship with the state security would become one of harassment, confrontation, and reprisal.

After this break with the Stasi, she wrote, she was not able to tell her friends about her previous secret meetings for fear of rejection. Over the next sixteen years, she succeeded in suppressing almost all memory of the collaboration. During this time she made a political about-face, devoting herself to working for the opposi-

tion. *This activity did not go unnoticed by the Stasi. As she related in February 1991 during her interview for this book, the Stasi set her up for arrest by putting into her possession forbidden printed material from the West. The official reason for her conviction was "accomplice to illegal association with people in West Berlin." For this crime she served a nine-month prison sentence.*

However, imprisonment did not deter her after her release from working to bring about a functioning socialism—efforts which, after the Wende, *earned her a seat in Parliament as a member of the United Left in coalition with the* PDS. *During discussions of the relationship between the Stasi and the Socialist Unity Party that occurred within the* PDS, *she became aware of the importance of working through this troubling episode in* GDR *history, both personally and collectively. She joined Parliament member Rainer Börner (*PDS*) and others who pleaded for open acknowledgment of all past Stasi connections in order to create a public forum for discussion of this problem in a differentiated way. To spur the discussion, she requested that the Stasi commission release her "perpetrator file" (*Täterin-Akte*) and wrote the first of her essays, "The White Spot on My Black Vest," in which she confronted her own Stasi past.*

What Jutta Braband learned from the Stasi commission so shook her that she again took the opportunity to write publicly, this time to step down from her position in the Bundestag. *The examination of her file by the Stasi commission disclosed that her performance had been considered "highly satisfactory," a discovery that was "a tremendous shock" to her. She now realized that what she had considered to be harmless conversations might well have contributed to the arrest and conviction of at least three people she knew. She admitted that her own persecution by the Stasi did not excuse what she had done.*

She feared that most people would not try to understand why she had participated or why she had broken contact. Most would not be interested in learning about her passionate involvement with the opposition during the sixteen years that followed. However, for her those sixteen years were of greater consequence than the five years of youthful idealism which motivated her to cooperate with the state. Still, she did not want to divide her life neatly into a "before" and "after" because it all belonged to her biography, even the contradictions. She reminded her audience that it was important to ask "how all people in the GDR *lived." Remembering was, she stated, "strenuous, uncomfortable, painful," and it would not bring one popularity. Nevertheless, she urged other East Germans to speak out about their own past so that they might come to a better understanding of their role and responsibility in the "repressive system." Finally, she hoped that by resigning her position in Parliament, she could encourage open discussion about past personal involvement in sustaining the* SED*-state.*

*   *   *

The case of Jutta Braband illustrates the blurring of boundaries between perpetrator and victim, for she was both. Her story makes clear that the question of judgment is very difficult. There are no easy answers or clear-cut distinctions when it comes to comprehending the situation of someone who consciously and willfully passed on information to the secret police, then later completely changed her position.

To demand a differentiated evaluation of those who collaborated with any level of the state apparatus—particularly, but not exclusively, the state security—is not to call for a blanket amnesty, as was considered by some politicians and public officials just after unification. It cannot be ignored that some people made decisions and took actions that caused suffering for many GDR *citizens who simply dared to disagree openly with the Party. Not demanding accountability would imply to victims and victims' families that their suffering was inconsequential. Grouping all collaborators together as villains of equal magnitude, however, is just as inappropriate.*

Jutta Braband's story demonstrates the need for discriminating thought when trying as an outsider to comprehend anything about the GDR, *from the workings of the Stasi to the social policies for women. With this book, we hope to contribute to that kind of differentiated understanding.*

CHRONOLOGY
AND
GLOSSARY

Dates

October 7, 1989. Fortieth anniversary of the German Democratic Republic. Nonviolent protest demonstrations in East Berlin, Leipzig, Dresden, Jena, and other cities were met with heavy police violence which continued on October 8.

November 4, 1989. Five-hundred thousand East Germans gathered at Alexanderplatz in East Berlin to demonstrate for democratic reform. Largest unofficial demonstration in GDR history. Speakers included prominent writers such as Christa Wolf, Stefan Heym, and Christoph Hein, as well as major figures in the Party, such as Gregor Gysi, Markus Wolf, and Günter Schabowski.

November 9, 1989. Opening of the Berlin Wall. Impetus was the announcement by Secretary for Information Günter Schabowski on the GDR evening news that permission to travel beyond GDR borders would be expedited.

March 18, 1990. First free *Volkskammer* (People's Chamber) elections in the GDR, with 93% voter turnout. The conservative CDU coalition won 48% of the vote; the SPD 22%; the PDS 16%; the "Liberals" 5%; the Coalition 90, 3%; Greens and Autonomous Women's Association (UFV), 2%; United Left, 0.25%; DFD, 0.25%, others, 3.5%.

May 6, 1990. First free local elections in the GDR.

July 2, 1990. "Monetary union," the first stage of German unification. The East German Mark was replaced by the West German deutsch Mark.

October 3, 1990. German unification or "political union."

December 2, 1990. First elections for all of Germany. The CDU coalition won in all of the new federal states except Brandenburg.

Terms

ABM (*Arbeitsbeschaffungsmaßnahmen*). A work program created by the federal government, generally lasting one or two years. Many of these positions were phased out in the summer of 1992.

Alexanderplatz. Main square in the center of East Berlin.

Arbeiter- und Bauernfakultät. Educational reform in the early years of the GDR which aimed to make higher degrees more readily available to those people whose education was interrupted by World War II or to those who did not have the academic preparation of an elite bourgeois background.

ARD. West German television network.

Aufbau Verlag. Major publishing house in the GDR.

Autonomous Women's Association (*Unabhängiger Frauenverband*, UFV). Umbrella organization for numerous women's organizations, founded in December 1989.

Babelsberg. District in Potsdam that served as headquarters for the German film industry before World War II and then for state-controlled GDR film production until 1990.

Baby-Jahr (baby year). A year of paid maternity leave available to single mothers and mothers with more than one child. Married mothers received twenty-six weeks of leave for the first child.

Berliner Ensemble. Theater in East Berlin known especially for its productions of plays by East Berlin playwright Bertolt Brecht (1898–1956).

Berufsverbot. Government prohibition against gainful employment in one's profession.

Biermann, Wolf. Politically outspoken singer-songwriter. His expatriation from the GDR in 1976 signaled a turning point in GDR cultural policy. Many artists and intellectuals experienced repression after protesting the action against Biermann.

Block party. Any of the East German political parties other than the SED. They were known by this term because all cast their vote in a unanimous "block" with the ruling Party, the SED.

Bohley, Bärbel. Artist and strong advocate for human rights and democratic reform during the *Wende*. Founding member of Women for Peace in 1982 and New Forum in 1989.

Bonzen. Party "bosses" or people with high profiles in the SED.

Brandenburg. Region surrounding Berlin; one of the five new federal states. Potsdam is its capital.

BRD (*Bundesrepublik Deutschland*). Federal Republic of Germany (FRG). Formerly West Germany. Now the name for unified Germany.

Bündnis 90. *See* Coalition 90.

Bundestag. The larger body of the bicameral Parliament of the Federal Republic before and after unification.

Cafe Kranzler. Historic cafe on Kurfürstendamm, symbol of West Berlin affluence.

CDU (*Christlich-Demokratische Unions*). Christian Democratic Union—block party in the GDR and conservative party in the FRG. The CDU-coalition won heavily in the first free GDR *Volkskammer* elections (March 18, 1990), as well as in the first all-German elections (December 2, 1990).

Charité. Largest hospital in East Berlin, founded by Frederick the Great.

Checkpoint Charlie. Border check point between East and West Berlin used for non-Germans until East German border restrictions were lifted in November 1989.

Chemnitz. City in Saxony, called Karl-Marx-Stadt in the days of the GDR.

Coalition 90 (*Bündnis 90*). Coalition of citizens groups founded during the *Wende* to promote socialist democracy, including New Forum, Democracy Now, and Initiative for Human Rights.

CSU (*Christlich-Soziale Union*). Christian Social Union, conservative party in coalition with the CDU.

DDR (*Deutsche Demokratische Republik*). German Democratic Republic (GDR), East Germany.

DEFA. East German Film Productions, film studios in Babelsberg, GDR.

DFD (*Demokratischer Frauenbund Deutschlands*). Official organization for women in the GDR.

DFF (*Deutscher Fernsehfunk*). State-controlled East German television.

Dresden. Capital city of Saxony.

EOS (*Erweiterte Oberschule*). University-preparatory high school in the GDR.

Exquisitenläden. Shops in the GDR where goods imported from East Bloc countries could be bought for GDR currency.

FDGB (*Freier Deutscher Gewerkschaftsbund*). The GDR's labor union.

FDJ (*Freie Deutsche Jugend*). Official socialist youth organization in the GDR.

Frauenhaus Bora. Shelter for battered women in East Berlin sponsored by the Protestant church, founded in 1990.

Frauenpolitik. Economic and social policies affecting women.

FRG (Federal Republic of Germany). Name for the West German state founded in 1949 and name of all of Germany since unification.

Friedrichshain. District of East Berlin.

GDR (German Democratic Republic). Name for the East German state founded in 1949.

Glienicke Bridge. Bridge spanning the Havel River on the southwest border between West Berlin and Potsdam. Not a border crossing point, the bridge was used for the exchange of prisoners between East and West and other military operations during the Cold War.

Greens. West German grass-roots environmental party. Spread to the eastern part of Germany after unification.

Gysi, Gregor. East Berlin attorney. Chosen as head of the SED on December 12, 1989, and continued as head of SED successor party, Party for Democratic Socialism (PDS).

Haushaltstag (household day in the GDR). One working day off per month to all married women, to single women with children under the age of sixteen, and to women over forty without children.

Heimat. Homeland or country of one's heritage.

Henschel. Largest publishing house in the GDR.

Heym, Stefan. Well-known GDR writer. His writings became increasingly critical of the SED.

HO (*Handelsorganisation*). State-owned retail business or restaurant.

Honecker, Erich. General Secretary of the SED and functional head of the GDR from 1971 until October 18, 1989.

Initiative for Peace and Human Rights (IFM). Oppositional organization founded in 1985 in the GDR.

Intershops. Shops in the GDR where Western goods could be bought for Western currency.

Kaderakte. The confidential file kept by the state security (Stasi) in which were recorded the professional and political activities of GDR citizens.

Ka De We (*Kaufhaus des Westens*). Department store in West Berlin.

Kindergarten. Tuition-free state day care for children between the ages of three and five.

Kindergeld. Monthly sum paid by the government to families with children.

Kinderkrippe. Tuition-free state nursery care for children under the age of three.

Kohl, Helmut. Became Chancellor of the Federal Republic of Germany in 1982. As head of the CDU, he was a major force in forging unification.

Köppe, Ingrid. Founding member of New Forum and a representative to the Round Table. Nominated as a Coalition 90/Greens representative to the *Bundestag* from the new federal state of Saxony-Anhalt.

Krenz, Egon. Member of the Politbüro in the GDR, in charge of Security, Youth, and Sports. Succeeded Erich Honecker and served as General Secretary of the SED and head of the GDR from October 18, 1989, until December 6, 1989.

Kurfürstendamm. Boulevard in West Berlin and a major shopping area.

LDPD (*Liberal-Demokratische Partei Deutschlands*). Liberal-Democratic Party of Germany. One of the GDR's block parties, known as the "Liberals."

Leipzig. City in Saxony and site of the peace vigils that began in 1980 and grew to large protest demonstrations in the fall of 1989.

Liebknecht, Karl (1871–1919). Leading figure in the Spartakus workers' movement, a forerunner to the German Communist Party (KDP), established in 1919.

Magistrat. Interim governing body for East Berlin formed in May 1990 and dissolved after the all-German elections on December 2, 1990.

Marzahn. District on the eastern extreme of East Berlin known for its numerous prefabricated high-rise apartment buildings.

Modrow, Hans. Head of the SED for Dresden until he became Minister-President of the GDR on November 13, 1989. He served in that capacity until the *Volkskammer* elections on March 18, 1990.

Muttipolitik. GDR policies that aimed to benefit mothers.

Nefertiti. Famous bust in the Egyptian museum in West Berlin.

Neubauwohnungen. Prefabricated high-rise apartments of relatively uniform design.

Neues Deutschland. The Party's official daily newspaper.

New federal states. Term used since unification to refer to the territory of the former GDR. The five new states are Brandenburg, Mecklenburg-Western Pomerania, Saxony, Saxony-Anhalt, Thuringia.

New Forum. Influential, immensely popular, prodemocracy movement in the GDR. Established in September 1989.

Nikolai Quarter. Historic area in the center of East Berlin, which was renovated as a shopping area just before the opening of the Wall.

Old federal states. Term used since unification to refer to the territory of the former FRG. The eleven old states are Baden-Württemberg, Bavaria, Berlin, Bremen, Hamburg, Hesse, Lower Saxony, North Rhine-Westphalia, Rhineland-Palatinate, Saarland, Schleswig-Holstein.

"Ossis." "Easties," slang term for residents of the former GDR.

Paragraph 218. Paragraph of West German criminal code of 1871 which made abortion on demand illegal if a woman could not prove fetal deformity, rape or incest, danger to the health of the mother, or socioeconomic hardship. Women's groups and human rights activists crusaded after the *Wende* for adoption of the GDR's more liberal policy of 1972, which made abortion legal on demand within the first trimester. Consultation with a physician was required in both German states for an abortion after the first trimester.

[The] Party. Common GDR term used to refer to the Socialist Unity Party, the SED.

PDS (*Partei des Demokratischen Sozialismus*). Party of Democratic Socialism. Successor party to the SED after the *Wende.*

Politbüro. Highest governing body in the GDR.

Poppe, Ulrike. Founding member of Women for Peace in the Protestant church in 1982 and founding member of the Initiative for Peace and Human Rights in 1985. In 1989 she became a spokesperson for Democracy Now, a prodemocracy organization in the GDR.

Potsdamer Platz. Bustling center of Berlin before World War II. After 1961 it became a vast vacant strip of no man's land between the outer and inner walls that enclosed West Berlin.

Prenzlauer Berg. District of East Berlin, home to many artists.

Ravensbrück. Nazi death camp.

Reich, Jens. Molecular biologist and well-known dissident.

Reisekader. Term for people allowed to travel outside the GDR and the East Bloc.

Rostock. Coastal city in Mecklenburg-Western Pomerania.

Round Table. Unofficial, multiconstituency advisory body to the interim government of Hans Modrow, November 1989 to March 1990.

Schabowski, Günter. Secretary for Information for the SED. Editor-in-chief of the SED newspaper *Neues Deutschland* until 1985. He announced on November 9, 1989, during the Tenth Plenum of the Central Committee that permission to travel outside the GDR would be expedited. This announcement was aired on the GDR evening news.

SED (*Sozialistische Einheitspartei Deutschlands*). Socialist Unity Party of Germany. Ruling party in the GDR, often referred to as "the Party." During the *Wende* it was dissolved and reconstituted as the PDS.

Skinheads. German youth in eastern and western Germany, some of whom are affiliated with the neo-Nazis, who commit violence against Jews and foreigners with dark skin.

SPD (*Sozialdemokratische Partei Deutschlands*). Social Democratic Party of Germany. Second largest of the two major parties in West Germany after the CDU.

Staatsbürgerkunde. Course of study in GDR schools concerned primarily with Marxist-Leninist political education.

Stasi. Common term for the Ministry for State Security or *Staatssicherheit.*

Tisch, Harry. Head of the state-administered labor union, FDGB. Sentenced to eighteen months' probation in June 1991 for misappropriation of funds as a GDR leader.

Trabant or **Trabi.** Small two-stroke automobile manufactured in the GDR. Very expensive and could only be acquired new after a wait which might be from eight to twenty years.

UFA. German film studies in Babelsberg before the founding of the German Democratic Republic.

United Left. Small party that worked in coalition with the PDS after earning seats in the first all-German Parliament.

Volkskammer. People's Chamber, the largest of the GDR governing bodies. The five hundred representatives served five-year terms.

Wartburg. Automobile manufactured in the GDR, slightly larger than the Trabant.

Weimar. City in Thuringia and capital of Germany during the Weimar Republic (1919–1933).

Wende. "Turn" or "change." Refers to the events in the GDR surrounding the opening of the German-German border and the collapse of the SED government.

Weissensee. District in the northern part of East Berlin.

"Wessis." "Westies," slang term for residents from the former FRG.

West. Refers to West Germany or other "western" European or North American nations.

WiG. Women in German. American professional organization for feminists in German and German Studies.

Wolf, Christa. Leading GDR author, with extensive readership outside the GDR.

Wolf, Markus. Deputy Minister for State Security in the GDR.

Women for Peace. One of the early oppositional movements established in 1982 within the Protestant church in the GDR.

Young Pioneers (*Pionierorganisation "Ernst Thälmann"*). Socialist youth organization in the GDR for children through the seventh grade.

SELECTED BIBLIOGRAPHY

Aufbrüche, Dokumentation zur Wende in der DDR *(Oktober 1989 bis März 1990).* Ed. Goethe-Institut München and Herder-Institut Leipzig. München: Goethe Institut, 1991.

Bahr, Gisela. "Dabeigewesen: Tagebuchnotizen vom Winter 1989/90." *Women in German Yearbook 7.* Ed. Jeanette Clausen and Sara Friedrichsmeyer. Lincoln: University of Nebraska Press, 1991.

Bahrmann, Hannes, and Peter-Michael Fritsch. *Sumpf, Privilegien, Amtsmißbrauch, Schiebergeschäfte.* Berlin: LinksDruck Verlag, 1990.

Bahrmann, Hannes, and Christoph Links. *Wir sind das Volk. Die* DDR *zwischen 7. Oktober und 17. Dezember 1989. Eine Chronik.* Berlin: Aufbau, 1990.

Berghahn, Sabine, and Andrea Fritzsche. *Frauenrechte im Übergang, Rechtssituation von Frauen im* DDR- *und* BRD-*Recht sowie im Übergangsrecht.* Berlin: BasisDruck Verlagsgesellschaft, 1991.

Böhme, Irene. "Die Frau und der Sozialismus," *Die da drüben.* Berlin: Rotbuch, 1983. 82–107.

Braband, Jutta. "Der weiße Fleck auf meiner schwarzen Weste." *Neues Deutschland* (18 September 1991): 9.

———. "Jutta Braband (PDS/LL) zur Niederlegung ihres Bundestagsmandats nach der Überprüfung durch die Gauck-Behörde: 'Riesiges Erschrecken, wie die Stasi sich meiner bedienen konnte.'" *Neues Deutschland* (21 Februar 1992).

———. "Warum habe ich so lange geschwiegen?" *Die Zeit* 10 (6 März 1992): 15.

Chronik der Ereignisse in der DDR. Köln: Verlag Wissenschaft und Politik, 1989.

Dahn, Daniel, and Fritz Kopka, eds. *Und diese verdammte Ohnmacht. Report der unabhängigen Untersuchungskommission zu den Ereignissen vom 7./8. Oktober 1989 in Berlin.* Berlin: BasisDruck Verlagsgesellschaft, 1991.

"Dialog: Kein Einigland von Schwestern—West-Emanzen und Ost-Muttis." *Ypsilon* 1.5 (Spring 1991): 18.

Die DDR *stellt sich vor.* Berlin: Panorama DDR, 1986.

Dölling, Irene. "Alte und neue Dilemmata: Frauen in der ehemaligen DDR," *Women in German Yearbook 7.* Ed. Jeanette Clausen and Sara Friedrichsmeyer. Lincoln: University of Nebraska Press, 1991. 121–36.

———. "Between Hope and Helplessness—Women in the GDR after the 'Turning Point.'" *Feminist Review* (Autumn 1991): 3–15.

———. "Culture and Gender," *The Quality of Life in the German Democratic Republic: Changes and Developments in a State Socialist Society.* Ed. Marilyn Rueschemeyer and Christine Lemke. Trans. Michel Vale. Armonk: M.E. Sharpe, 1989. 27–47.

Eckart, Gabriele. *So sehe ick die Sache (Protokolle).* Köln: Kiepenheuer und Witsch, 1984.

Fischer, Erica, and Petra Lux. *Ohne uns ist kein Staat zu machen. DDR-Frauen nach der Wende.* Köln: Kiepenheuer & Witsch, 1990.

Förster, Peter, and Günter Roski. *DDR zwischen Wende und Wahl. Meinungsforscher analysieren den Umbruch.* Berlin: LinksDruck Verlag, 1990.

Friedrich-Ebert-Stiftung, ed. *Frauen in der DDR, Auf dem Weg zur Gleichberechtigung?* Bonn: Verlag Neue Gesellschaft, 1987.

Glässner, Gert-Joachim. *Der schwierige Weg zur Demokratie, Vom Ende der DDR zur deutschen Einheit.* Opladen: Westdeutscher Verlag, 1991.

Gysi, Jutta, ed. *Familienleben in der DDR: Zum Alltag von Familien mit Kindern.* Berlin: Akademie-Verlag, 1989.

Hein, Eva, and Klaus Rosenfeld. *Frauen in Ausbildung und Beruf.* Berlin: Staatsverlag der DDR, 1985.

Holschuh, Albrecht. "Protokollsammlungen der DDR." *German Studies Review* 15.2 (May 1992): 267–87.

Kahlau, Cordula, ed. *Aufbruch! Frauenbewegung in der DDR. Dokumentation.* München: Verlag Frauenoffensiv, 1990.

Kaufmann, Eva. "DDR-Schriftstellerinnen, die Widersprüche und die Utopie." *Women in German Yearbook 7.* Ed. Jeanette Clausen and Sara Friedrichsmeyer. Lincoln: University of Nebraska Press, 1991. 109–20.

Kirsch, Sara. *Die Pantherfrau: Fünf unfrisierte Erzählungen aus dem Kassetten-Recorder.* Berlin and Weimar: Aufbau, 1973.

Kleines politisches Wörterbuch. Berlin: Dietz Verlag, 1967, 1983.

Klier, Freya. *Lüg, Vaterland. Erziehung in der DDR.* München: Kindler Verlag, 1990.

Königsdorf, Helga. *Adieu DDR: Protokolle eines Abschieds.* Reinbek bei Hamburg: Rowohlt, 1990.

Kolinsky, Eva. *Women in Contemporary Germany: Life, Work, and Politics.* Providence and Oxford: Berg Publishers, 1993.

Koschinski, Kirk, Bernd Musiolek, and Carola Wuttke, eds. *Parteien und politische Bewegungen im letzten Jahr der DDR (Oktober 1989 bis April 1990).* Berlin: Basis-Druck Verlagsgesellschaft, 1991.

Kuhrig, Herta, and Wulfram Speigner, eds. *Wie emanzipiert sind die Frauen in der DDR?* Köln: Pahl-Rugenstein, 1979.

Kukutz, Irene, and Katja Havemann. *Geschützte Quelle.* Berlin: BasisDruck Verlagsgesellschaft, 1990.

Kulke, Christine, Heidi Kopp-Degethoff, and Ulrike Ramming, eds. *Wider das schlichte Vergessen: Der Deutsch-Deutsche Einigungsprozess. Frauen im Dialog.* Berlin: Orlanda Frauenverlag, 1992.

Lau, Karin, and Karlheinz Lau, eds. *Deutschland auf dem Weg zur Einheit. Dokumente einer Revolution.* Braunschweig: Westermann, 1990.

Lemke, Christiane. "Beyond the Ideological Stalemate: Women & Politics in the FRG and the GDR in Comparison." *German Studies Review,* DAAD special issue (1990): 87–96.

Maaz, Hans-Joachim. *Der Gefühlsstau. Ein Psychogramm der DDR.* Berlin: Argon, 1990.

MacKinnon, Catharine A. *Toward a Feminist Theory of the State.* Cambridge: Harvard UP, 1989.

Menge, Marlies. *Ohne uns läuft nichts mehr: die Revolution in der DDR.* Stuttgart: Deutsche Verlags-Anstalt, 1990.

Mitter, Armin, and Stefan Wolle, eds. *Ich liebe euch doch alle! Befehle und Lageberichte des MfS, Januar–November 1989.* Berlin: BasisDruck Verlagsgesellschaft, 1990.

Mocker, Elke, Beate Rüther, and Birgit Sauer. "Frauen- und Familienpolitik: Wie frauenfreundlich war die DDR?" *Deutschland Archiv* 45.1 (September 1990): 1700–1705.

Mudry, Anna, ed. *Gute Nacht, du Schöne.* Frankfurt am Main: Luchterhand, 1991.

Musall, Bettina, " 'Viele dachten, die spinnen,' Lage und Niederlage der Frauen im vereinten Deutschland." *Der Spiegel* (18 März 1991): 68–84.

Mushaben, Joyce. "Paying the Price of German Unification: Männer planen, Frauen baden aus." *GDR Bulletin* 17.2 (Fall 1991): 3–9.

Nickel, Hildegard Maria. "Frauen in der DDR." *Aus Politik und Zeitgeschichte.* Supplement to the newspaper *Das Parlament,* nos. 16–17 (1990): 41–42.

———. "Women in the GDR: Will Renewal Pass Them By?" *Women in German Yearbook 6.* Ed. Jeanette Clausen and Helen Cafferty. Lanham, NY: University Press of America, 1991. 99–108.

———. "Sex-Role Socialization in Relationships as a Function of the Division of Labor: A Sociological Explanation for the Reproduction of Gender Differences." *The Quality of Life in the German Democratic Republic: Changes and Developments in a State Socialist Society.* Ed. Marilyn Rueschemeyer and Christine Lemke. Trans. Michel Vale. Armonk: M.E. Sharpe, 1989. 48–58.

Oelschlegel, Vera. *"Wenn das meine Mutter wüßt . . ." Selbstporträt.* Berlin: Ullstein, 1991.

Panorama DDR—Do You Know about the GDR? Dresden: Grafischer Großbetrieb Völkerfreundschaft, 1983.

Panorama DDR—Sozialpolitik. Dresden: Grafischer Großbetrieb Völkerfreundschaft, 1987.

Prausa, Eva-Maria. "Reprivatization in the ex-GDR." Trans. Pam Allen. Unpublished manuscript of lecture given at Hamilton College, New York, March 1991.

Projekte mit von für Frauen in und um Leipzig—1991. Ed. Rat der Stadt Leipzig. Leipzig: Leipziger Verlags-und Druckereigesellschaft GmbH, 1991.

Röth, Uta. "Die klassenlose Gretchenfrage. Über die Vereinbarkeit von Beruf und Familie." *Wir wollen mehr als ein Vaterland.* Ed. Gislinde Schwarz and Christine Zenner. Reinbek bei Berlin: Rowohlt, 1990. 132–44.

Rohnstock, Katrin, and Astrid Luthardt, eds. *Handbuch. Wegweiser für Frauen in den fünf neuen Bundesländern.* Berlin: BasisDruck Verlagsgesellschaft, 1991.

Rosenberg, Dorothy. "Shock Therapy: GDR Women in Transition from a Socialist Welfare State to a Social Market Economy." *Signs* 17.1 (Autumn 1991): 129–51.

———. "The Emancipation of Women in Fact and Fiction: Images and Role Models in GDR Literature." *Women, State, and Party in Eastern Europe.* Ed. Sharon Wolchik and Alfred Meyer. Durham: Duke University Press, 1985.

Rüddenklau, Wolfgang, and Peter Grimm, eds. *DDR-Opposition 1986–1989. Dokumentiert aus den "Umweltblättern."* Berlin: BasisDruck Verlagsgesellschaft, 1991.

Rueschemeyer, Marilyn, and Christine Lemke, eds. *The Quality of Life in the German Democratic Republic: Changes and Developments in a State Socialist Society.* Trans. Michel Vale. Armonk: M.E. Sharpe, 1989.

Rueschemeyer, Marilyn, and Hanna Schissler. "Women in the two Germanys." *German Studies Review.* DAAD special issue. (1990): 71–85.

Runge, Irene. *Ausland DDR: Fremdenhaß.* Berlin: Dietz, 1990.

Schmitt, Walfriede. "Der Reichtum, der in dir steckt," *Ypsilon. Zeitschrift aus Frauensicht* 4 (April 1991): 4–7.

Schönemann, Sibylle, dir. *Die verriegelte Zeit,* 1990. Film distributed by Internationes. English trans: *Locked-Up Time.*

Schorlemmer, Friedrich. "Vom Aufbruch zum Ausverkauf. Ein Jahr nach dem Ende der Mauer: Eine ostdeutsche Bilanz." *Die Zeit* 46 (9 November 1990): 52.

Schüddekopf, Charles, ed. *"Wir sind das Volk!" Flugschriften. Aufrufe und Texte einer deutschen Revolution.* Reinbek bei Hamburg: Rowohlt, 1990.

Schwarz, Gislinde. "Das Ende der Mutti-Politik?" *Emma* (January 1991): 46.

Schwarz, Gislinde, and Christine Zenner, eds. *Wir wollen mehr als ein "Vaterland." DDR-Frauen im Aufbruch.* Reinbek bei Hamburg: Rowohlt, 1990.

Sillge, Ursula. *Un-Sichtbare Frauen. Lesben und ihre Emanzipation in der DDR.* Berlin: LinksDruck Verlag, 1991.

Staritz, Dietrich. *Abweicher. Verräter. Staatsfeinde. Opposition in der DDR. 1945–1990.* München: dtv Dokumente, 1991.

Statistisches Taschenbuch der DDR. 1989. Berlin: Staatsverlag der DDR, 1989.

Stephan, Cora, ed. *Wir Kollaborateure. Der Westen und die deutschen Vergangenheiten.* Reinbek bei Hamburg: Rowohlt, 1992.

Stratenschulte, Eckart. *DDR. Fragen und Antworten.* Berlin: Landeszentrale für politische Bildungsarbeit, 1986.

Wander, Maxie. *Guten Morgen, du Schöne.* Darmstadt: Luchterhand, 1979.

Winkler, Gunnar, ed. *Frauenreport '90.* Berlin: Verlag die Wirtschaft, 1990.

———. *Sozialreport '90: Daten und Fakten zur sozialen Lage in der DDR.* Berlin: Verlag die Wirtschaft, 1990.

Zentraler Ausschuß für Jugendweihe in der Deutschen Demokratischen Republik, ed. *Vom Sinn unseres Lebens.* Berlin: Verlag Neues Leben, 1983.

Zimmer, Dieter E. "Was 'n kleinkariertes Volk. Interview mit Helga Schütz." *Die Zeit* (3 Mai 1991): 24.